MOZART

and his world

MOZART

and his world

BY ERICH VALENTIN

A STUDIO BOOK

THE VIKING PRESS · NEW YORK

Letter from Leopold Mozart reporting the birth of his son Wolfgang Amadeus on 9th February 1756

When a child prodigy, Mozart accepted all the admiration accorded to his artistry with complete and unabashed self-possession. At nineteen he noted, with pride and satisfaction, fully conscious of his own powers, the 'terrific' noise of clapping, which accompanied every aria in his opera *La Finta Giardiniera* during its first performance at Munich. But when, in 1791, his *Magic Flute* was first presented in the Freihaus theatre in Vienna, he was most gratified by the 'silent applause'.

These three different reactions are symbolic of the growth and change in Mozart's personality. But perhaps the thing which is most attractive and mysterious about his short, full life is the contrast between his prosaic, down-to-earth quality as a man and the light and warmth of his radiant, almost prodigal, artistic character. He lived in a period of profound changes which were mounting to a climax. His life, in fact, represents the bridge between the

From Fischach and Aretsried the Mozart family moved to Pfersee near Augsburg

sheltered existence of a Bach, secure in a lifetime of devotion to the service of God, and the unceasing, God-questing unquiet of a Beethoven. We know from his letters that Mozart accepted the characteristic features of his era with clear-sighted knowledge of the world. He did not accomplish his life-work in a vacuum but was fully aware of his own value and function. Indeed, he did what his self-confident father, who despite his self-confidence was fully convinced of the essential superiority of the nobility, would never have dared to do: even to his superiors in rank he insisted on his rights as a man and his authority as an artist.

The famous phrase with which he terminated his quarrel with Count Arco, agent of the Salzburg Archbishop Hieronymus (whom, incidentally, Mozart

David Mozart of Pfersee
was granted civic rights in Augsburg in 1643

certainly misunderstood) shows this clearly. When he said to him: 'The heart ennobles the man,' it was not merely a taunt elicited by anger but a deeply-felt expression of the Rousseau doctrine which was then inspiring the younger generation. The same is true of Mozart's remark to von Langenmantel in October 1777 when the latter decorated him with an Order awarded him by the Pope: 'I could sooner acquire all your Orders than you could become what I am.'

This affair was particularly remarkable in that it took place not in Court circles but in an essentially middle-class town, Augsburg, where Mozart's father was born and bred and where the Mozart family had possessed civic rights since the seventeenth century. But the very contrast between this particular Mozart and the background of his ancestors, craftsmen who had quitted Pfersee, leaving their 'chattels' behind them, to seek the protection of the largest town in the area as early as the fourteenth century, brings out the extraordinary singularity of this Mozart's career. Allegiance to their home

The Mozart family lived in Augsburg from the seventeenth century onward

His father and local traditions had combined to tie his Bavarian-Swabian family to their native region. Mozart's father, born in 1719 to Johann Georg Mozart, a book-binder, was the first to break this tradition. He had received a comprehensive classical education at St Salvador's College. Nothing indicated that his musical gifts, which he found opportunities of putting to the test both at church and in private houses, would determine his career and eventually win the admiration and respect of professional musicians. Nor is there anything to tell us what caused him so to neglect his academic studies at the Alma Benedictina in Salzburg, after he had passed his Baccalauréat examination, that he was expelled; he seems on all other occasions to have been a strikingly conscientious and thorough person. Perhaps his self-will drove him to take some different course from that prescribed for him by others. Perhaps his love of music was stronger than his love of philosophy, particularly since, it appears, his appetite for knowledge was by no means as satisfied as he had anticipated it would be by the offerings of the university, an institution which was at that time greatly in need of reform.

Suddenly, he decided to join the orchestra of Count Thurn-Valassina. Three years later he had already risen to the second desk of violins in the Court orchestra of Archbishop Leopold Firmian.

Henceforth Leopold Mozart made his home in Salzburg, seat of the ecclesiastical principality of the 'Bavarian district of the Holy Roman Empire of the German Nation'. In 1747, after a long courtship, he married Anna Maria Pertl of St Gilgen, a serene, happy woman, and with her created a world of his own in their lodgings in the Getreidegasse, over which he ruled with patriarchal conscientiousness. Although a clever, energetic man, he never, to his chagrin, rose beyond the position of deputy conductor, but in the Getreidegasse he could rule supreme. And so he shut all that was professional out of his home and chose his friends with great care. His professional associates, even the Court trumpeter and writer, Johann Andreas Schachtner, were kept away from the house as much as possible.

His works, mostly appealing to the popular taste, and his spiritual strivings were in curious contrast to the baroque milieu of Salzburg. Inclined towards the ideas of the Age of

The house in St Gilgen where Mozart's mother was born

Even today the château and park of Leopoldskron, constructed
by Archbishop Firmian, are reminiscent of Salzburg's golden age in the eighteenth century

Enlightenment, he absorbed North German literature, such as the works of
Gottsched and Gellert (surprisingly, in view of his devout Christianity) and
formed a literature circle with his Benedictine writer friends in the privacy
of his house. On the one hand, he was temperamentally rather suspicious and
dour; on the other, he was isolated from the commonalty of his fellows by
the great success of his violin manual (which was widely acclaimed as an
educational masterpiece expressing the spirit of the age). Nevertheless, neither
of these facts prevented him from enjoying his quiet social gatherings.
One can see from his friendships with various fellow-citizens, in particular
his landlord Lorenz Hagenauer, his spontaneous participation in amusements and diversions and above all his fondness for slightly sarcastic humour
that his character was not all gravity. However much his ambition turned
him towards the Court, which alone could grant success to an eighteenth-
century artist, in the privacy of his home he avoided association with

From 1747 the Mozarts lived on the third floor of the Hagenauers' house

men who had anything to do with Court life. Within his little empire his own will and command were paramount and his good-humoured, cheerful wife retreated into the background before his authority. For the period this was nothing unusual. In Goethe's father's house in Frankfurt, for instance, the paternal authority extended even to the small details of housekeeping and the same was true of the Mozart family. With a certain pedantry, but also with a touching care, the deputy-conductor arranged the day's menu, worried about the servants and laid down careful rules for the kitchen and cellar.

Today it is hard to understand why Anna Maria Mozart, a splendid person well disposed for gaiety at any time, should have spent her entire life in the shade. It comes as rather a shock to realise, when reading Mozart's life story, that one has heard almost nothing of her until the account of her death in 1778. It was only when her gaiety and cheerfulness were missing that she came into the limelight for the first time. Her youth had not been remarkably exciting before her marriage to the young musician from Augsburg. From then on her peaceful existence was dedicated to the fulfilment of household duties

Mozart's mother: Anna Maria Mozart   Mozart's father: Leopold Mozart

and the production of seven children, of whom five died shortly after birth. But the old, solid house in the Getreidegasse, then a busy thoroughfare, was presided over by a benevolent spirit. While Leopold Mozart, as a true pessimist, considered all men scoundrels and confined himself rigorously to his own circle of friends, his wife provided the necessary encouragement and impetus for life.

All in all, the Mozart household presents a picture of a comfortable, middle-class family, such as could have been found in any small cathedral town in the eighteenth century. Only the flattering perspective in which it is seen from the present-day viewpoint and the associations which now cling to the name 'Mozart' lift the family out of monotonous uniformity and narrowness. The fact that Leopold Mozart was elected a member of the Leipzig 'Society of Musical Studies', the success of his violin manual and the recognition accorded to him by Friedrich Wilhelm Marpurg of Berlin, were good for his disillusioned, slightly resentful spirit. And with public recognition came a general happiness which eventually influenced even his family life.

Salzburg in winter, as it might have looked 200 years ago when Mozart was born

Mozart   The artistic career and personal destiny of Wolfgang Amadeus Mozart can only be fully understood if one remembers the clear-cut character of his father, the first Mozart to venture before the public. In his mind his son was to achieve the final fulfilment of his own ambitions, a fulfilment which had been denied to him. Leopold Mozart's life work did, in fact, culminate in achievements of the children who survived, 'Nannerl' and Wolfgang Amadeus, five years younger, who had been born on the evening of 27th January 1756 in the family's lodgings. That later the father and son were estranged was a tragic ending to a genuine friendship between members of two generations. The middle-class rococo ideals of the elder Mozart were in opposition to the ideas of the new age, which found its creed in the humanism of Goethe's *Iphigenie* and later, of course, in Mozart's own *Seraglio* and *Magic Flute*.

Johannes Chrysostomus Wolfgang Theophilus (= Amadeus) Mozart
was baptized in the cathedral at Salzburg on 28th January 1756

The world of Mozart's childhood: the courtyard of the Hagenauers' house and the Kollegienkirche

The 'amazing' thing about Mozart is that he, the embodiment of everything that is unique and gifted, had to go through all the natural phases of development before reaching the height of his powers. His father's world and the baroque world which revealed itself at every step in Salzburg formed the backdrop against which his childhood was played out. While his mother pervaded the kitchen, his father strove with solicitous care to provide everything for his children which he judged important for their future. At the beginning of their lives it was through him and him alone that they gained their experience of the outside world.

This outside world meant, first, domestic life in the Getreidegasse, instinct as it was with Leopold Mozart's spirit. Then came the town of Salzburg which even today still reflects the broad, leisurely quality of the eighteenth century, despite modern additions — new buildings and twentieth-century bustle. At that period Salzburg was under the gentle rule of Sigismund von Schrattenbach, a man devoted to the arts. In the peace following several years of upheaval, music and the theatre flourished, particularly the university theatre which had long outgrown its purely academic traditions. As it was peacetime, attention could be turned to the graces of life. Court music, church music and the theatre attracted many great artists to the pretty little town dominated by the Mönchberg and the great fortress.

Wolfgang Mozart's early childhood was like that of any other boy. His gifts emerged spontaneously from his play and pleasures. As he listened curiously to his father giving music lessons to his sister Nannerl, he began to find it diverting to imitate what he heard being learned. And so occurred the astounding feats which charmed and amazed even his critical father. Here and there in the 'notebook' which Leopold kept of Nannerl's progress there are proud fatherly comments, such as that Wolfgang had learned a minuet 'in his fourth year'. Even before the boy was properly aware of the meaning of the notes on the page, he composed a 'piano concerto'. 'At first,' wrote Schachtner, 'we laughed at what appeared to be a page of nonsense, but then his papa began to study the theme, the notes, the composition; for a long time he hung over the music, stiff with attention; and finally tears, tears of amazement and joy, fell from his eyes.' The earliest surviving compositions of the five-year-old boy show that his father guided his first steps with great skill and care. From then on all Wolfgang's childish amusements had to be linked with music.

But the game developed into something serious. With unrelenting severity the father impressed upon his child, now that he was seen to be so out of the ordinary, the necessity for constant work, constant diligence and industry.

Mozart's first composition, written at five years old, and endorsed with a proud marginal note by his father

This was due partly to his feeling of responsibility, partly to his gratitude at being distinguished by God through the gift of his son. It is impossible to tell how much strain he put on the physical powers and mental receptivity of the child. Nevertheless, Mozart loved his father tenderly. Every evening, singing his mysterious 'oragna figa tafa', he kissed the end of Papa's nose before going to bed and promised 'always to keep him in a little glass box'.

At the beginning Leopold Mozart kept his four-year-old child's powers a secret, confiding in only his closest friends, as Schachtner's memoirs and other documents show. And the boy's first public appearance on 1st September 1761 was modest and unremarkable: he sang in the choir in Eberlin's *Sigismundus Hungariae Rex*, which was performed on the stage of the Academy Theatre.

Wolfgang Amadeus *(left)* and Nannerl in 1762 in their court clothes –
a striking contrast between youth and stiff finery

Leopold had his reasons for this reticence: the work learnt and practised in
the quiet of the home should first, he decided, be tested outside Salzburg.

The learning and practising went on, patiently, tenaciously. Nannerl's notebook and a second notebook which Leopold gave his son on his saint's day in
1762 show that 'Wolferl's' artistic education was systematically built up
according to his father's taste and will. His quick grasp soon developed into
a creative mastery. With the same pleasure and single-mindedness with which
he absorbed music he strove to increase his general knowledge. It is certain
that in reading, writing and arithmetic, as later in learning foreign languages,
the guiding influence was his father's teaching. When it came to arithmetic
Mozart showed the same enthusiasm that he had shown for music, and
demonstrated his childhood fervour by scribbling sums all over the tables,
chairs and walls.

On tour   The day of 12th January 1762 was an important one in Mozart's life. It
was the first time that the family set off on a tour. With this journey to

Munich began the long series of travels to this town and that town, this country and that country, which developed into a continual restlessness. From this time until 1781 when he settled in Vienna Wolfgang was, in all, fifteen years 'on the road', taking all his journeys together. It was a hard school in which to complete one's education.

The periods of peace permitted by Leopold Mozart's ambitious wanderlust were few indeed, and so Mozart's youth was largely spent among strangers. The significance of his journeyings is therefore greater than it might otherwise have been. For him they were the decisive years in which he learned his art and gained his experience of the world. In 1762 the Mozarts set out on their second journey, this time not to the Court of a small prince, like that in Munich, but to the Imperial Court. Unfortunately the kindness and praise of Emperor Franz I, a music lover, and the hardly less musical Empress Maria Theresa, could not disguise the fact that the amazement at the sensational sight of a young child playing, far outweighed the enlightened appreciation of a gift which was something more than sensational. More important than the Court performances was a meeting with one of the 'modern' musicians of the day, Georg Christoph Wagenseil. He taught music to the Empress and her daughter, Marie Antoinette, whom (so the legend goes) Mozart promised to marry because she had helped him up when he slipped on the polished floor. After this charming story it is sobering to remember that Marie Antoinette was later, as Queen of France, to die at roughly the same age as Mozart.

After Nannerl and Wolfgang, 'the clever, lively, charming Mozart', as Count Zinzendorf called him, had proved themselves before the nobility in Munich and Vienna,

Princess Marie Antoinette at the age of seven;
later, as Queen of France, she met her death on the guillotine

Salzburg's Court Chancellor,
Franz von Mölk

Lorenz Hagenauer, friend and
landlord of the Mozart family

they were presented by their father, who laid great stress on this kind of reputation, to the Prince, Archbishops and the Court at Salzburg. The children were allowed to be presented on the birthday of the Archbishop, 28th February 1763, when Leopold Mozart was given the position of deputy conductor. The Court diary reads: 'The young seven-year-old son and the ten-year-old *[sic]* daughter of the new Deputy conductor performed upon their instrument, the son also upon a violin'.

Mozart, who played keyboard instruments all his life, was an excellent pianist and improviser and felt equally at home with the organ, but was at this period only just beginning the violin. Schachtner tells how the seven-year-old boy, who had never even held a violin, begged to join in at a musical evening held by his father with a few friends at home. His father was not going to give him permission but at Schachtner's plea he gave way. 'Soon I saw with amazement that I was quite superfluous and I quietly put my violin away . . .' And he saw Mozart's equally astonished father 'with tears of wonder and happiness rolling down his cheeks at this scene'.

A wide chasm yawned between the sheltered family life in Salzburg and the tumultuous activity of the big world in which the children were dazzled by the bright light of publicity. That Mozart was not ruined by this dichotomy was due to his youth and his artistic seriousness. It is certainly legitimate to speak of seriousness. It stamps Mozart's features in all the portraits of him which are still extant. They all show that he looked older than he really was — even the first portrait which Leopold had painted of him and his sister by Lorenzoni in 1763: in it Mozart wears the 'gala dress' which the Empress had given him. His dignified bearing and mature expression hardly seem in keeping with his childish body.

His sensitive personality — as sensitive as his ear — made him very susceptible to every influence from outside. The continual to-ing and fro-ing, changes from excitement to placidity and the variety of surroundings and people had a profound effect on him. Moreover, his health varied greatly and from time to time he suffered with toothache and headaches, fevers and even serious illnesses. With all this it seems amazing that Mozart should always have been a happy cheerful child and, in fact, should have remained grateful for the gift of life to the end of his days, even though he contemplated death without fear.

His happiest hours were those spent at home between tours. Later, when he was in Vienna, he often called to mind the friends the Mozarts had had in Salzburg. They brought back memories of gay irresponsibility, times of spontaneous music-making and earnest discussions between Leopold Mozart and his scholarly friends about Gottsched or Wieland, a writer much read by the Mozarts, or music and drama. There were the Hagenauers who lived in the same house as the Mozarts, the Mölks, the Barisanis and most of the people who held some position in the town. Sometimes they would all walk out to Aigen where the Mozart parents were married, to Gnigl to visit the Robinigs or perhaps to see their cousin Pertl in Mülln. Daily life was diversified with card-games and air-gun shooting, to which Leopold Mozart was devoted, church-going and work. Sometimes they made excursions further afield, to Berchtesgaden or Seeau.

As in Mozart's day, the
sundial shows the hour in the Robinig house in Gnigl

Although Leopold Mozart came to dissociate himself with increasing irritation from the official life of the town, he nevertheless felt himself firmly rooted in it. The antipathy which was later, for different reasons, to cause both the son and the father to say hard words about Salzburg, could not prevent their thoughts from centring on it even if only to criticize the small-town gossip normal in a cathedral city of that kind. (In any case the latent tension between the Court and the town was one of Salzburg's historic traditions.)

As yet, Mozart's own will had not developed. He still saw life through his father's eyes. But in his mind he created a miniature fantasy-world in which his sister was allowed to share to a certain extent. The story of the 'Backwards Kingdom' which he told her was a foretaste of all the poetic outlets in which he later found expression for his ideas.

The great tour of Western Europe on which the Mozarts set out on 9th June 1763 brought with it the first signs of an independent, artistic and also personal judgment. During the tour the seeds were sown of that difference of opinion which led to a tragic conflict between father and son, generation and generation. For the first time during this three-year tour the Mozarts experienced not only tremendous success and admiring recognition, but also doubt and fear, worry over the world prodigy whom they exhibited.

At first everything looked hopeful. It was true that on the political horizon storm clouds were looming up which foreboded the war between Prussia and Austria, and that the publication of Rousseau's *Contrat Social* announced the

The Mozarts lodged
with Störzer,
landlord of the inn
'Zum Hirschen' in Munich

end of the old era and the beginning of a new one. But all that was only by the way as far as the family was concerned.

Full of expectation, the Mozarts set out on their journey westward. Munich, which Mozart later yearned after in vain more than once, received them with promising friendliness; Prince Max Joseph III, a great music enthusiast, and Duke Clement, gave high praise to the boy who played the piano and violin for them several times in the Nymphenburg Palace. But how much greater was Leopold's pride when his children were presented in Augsburg. With recommendations to Duke Carl Eugen they continued their journey through the beautiful fertile land round the city. But Leopold was vexed and disappointed to learn in Plochingen that the Duke was away hunting. They changed their plans and went to Ludwigsburg, via Cannstatt instead of Stuttgart. But in Ludwigsburg, a charming town with a fine castle, they had to be content with the Duke's Master of the Hunt and the chief conductor, Nicolo Jommelli. Leopold Mozart viewed Jommelli, a man who occupies an important position in the history of opera, with his all too easily aroused mistrust. It annoyed him that the Italian expressed amazement at finding so much 'musical genius and soul' in a 'child of German nationality'.

But soon afterwards Leopold's insulted spirit, offended by the 'superstitious' men with whom it came in contact, was soothed when the Mozarts had a great success in playing for the Princess Palatine in Schwetzingen.

There is nothing to tell us what effect this journey had on the mind of the person around whom it revolved. Nannerl's naively awkward sketches and

The great Italian
composer, Jommelli,
admired the genius
of the young Mozart
in Ludwigsburg

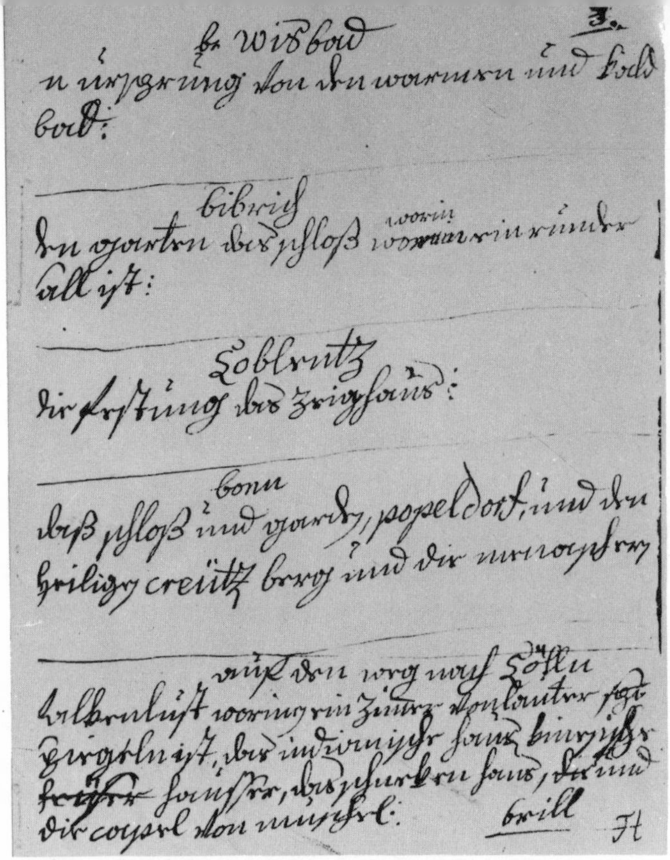

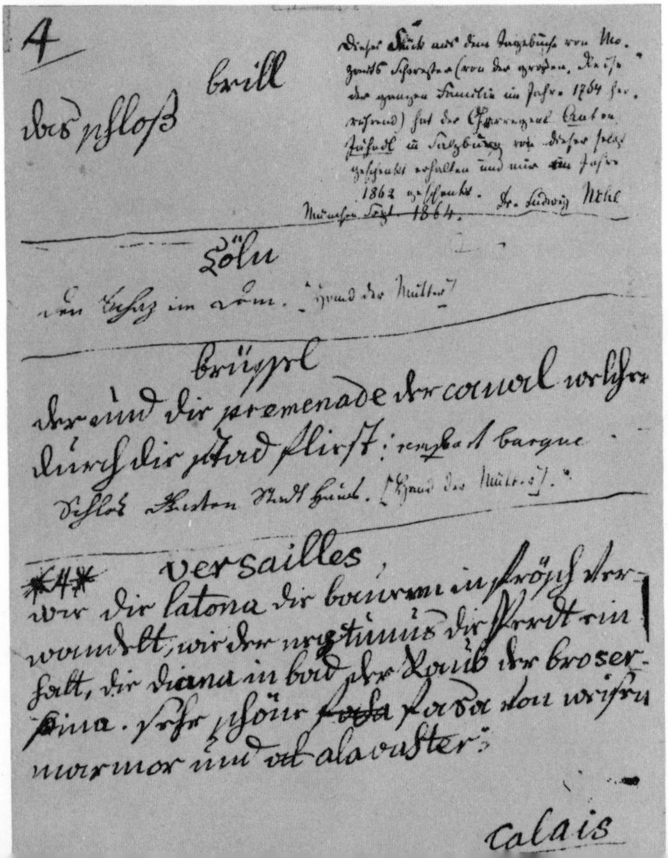

Nannerl kept a diary
of the places they
saw during the journey

Leopold's letters to his friend Hagenauer give, basically, only the external happenings. And yet several of these happenings were symbolic in their way — Mozart's first meeting with the world of Italian music in the person of Jommelli, and in Schwetzingen with the modern music of the day as played by the Mannheim Orchestra. Even Leopold Mozart could not prevent himself from expressing his pleasure at the solid achievements of the Mannheim musicians, combining the compliment with a passing jibe at some of his Salzburg colleagues.

It is interesting to note that Goethe, then fourteen years old, heard the seven-year-old Mozart in Frankfurt; and even more interesting to see that the public notice of the performance announced it more as a 'spectacle' than as a 'concert'. This was underlined by Leopold's practice of making his children, and particularly his son, not only play on the piano, violin and organ but also perform all kinds of tricks such as playing on a keyboard with a cloth held over it or undergoing various ear-tests, in contradiction of his beliefs and feelings as a teacher. The young

View of Brussels in the eighteenth century

Mozart became a sensation. And the elder one, disillusioned, finally reached the conclusion that his artistic abilities were overlooked on account of these spectacular inessentials.

During the journey from Mainz to Aachen they only rarely achieved what they had intended. Above all, Leopold would have preferred ducats to the kisses showered on Mozart by Princess Amalie, Frederick II's sister. Nannerl's diary of the journey tells of sightseeing in Bonn, Brühl and Cologne. Prince Karl of Lorraine, Field Marshal of the Austrian lowlands, angrily told Leopold Mozart that he (Karl) cared for nothing but 'hunting, guzzling and swilling', and kept the Salzburg party waiting for a long time before he allowed them to perform. They used this involuntary period of inactivity to visit the museums, churches and 'natural history collections'. But Rubens and Rembrandt were poor comfort to Leopold Mozart. He was worried about the well-being both of his children and of his purse. During this pause 'the quite extraordinarily cheerful' Wolfgang Amadeus sat himself down before his manuscript paper and composed.

Leopold looked to Paris to fulfil all their hopes and expectations. Paris —

Paris in 1763: Leopold Mozart with his children Wolfgang and Nannerl (standing behind the piano) playing at a concert

the metropolis, of whose approaching dangers Leopold informed Frau Hagenauer in a letter about Parisian women: 'Everyone does as he likes and (unless God be especially gracious to them) the state of France will go the way of the Persian Empire'. The French king, Louis XV, wearied by a series of political mishaps, lived on the past glory of his ancestors, whose splendid palace at Versailles provided a background for the highly successful concerts of the Mozart children. The charming Queen, the less charming but cleverer Madame de Pompadour and the royal children all enjoyed the performances given by the 'enfants prodiges' from Salzburg. Mozart dedicated his first work to be printed in Paris, the *Sonates pour le Clavecin,* to the modest Princesse Victoire.

The Mozarts reached the French Court through the good offices of a disciple of Gottsched, Melchior Grimm, a German who had lived in Paris for years and whose cool, incisive brain flourished in the brilliant atmosphere of the French city. With him Leopold Mozart laid aside all his suspicion and, overawed by his elegance and suavity, trusted him blindly. Wolfgang, on the other hand, openly mistrusted the man from the beginning and in later years his mistrust was proved to be well-founded.

Grimm, a friend of Diderot and Rousseau and a
champion of the Italian opera in the city of his adoption,
opened the doors to all the nobility and gentry of Paris.
There were concerts here, concerts there, presents by the
coachful, praises, caresses. Olivier painted the Prince de
Conti's tea-party, at which Mozart played, and Carmontelle immortalised father, son and daughter in a portrait
which was engraved by Delafosse so that it could be
widely distributed. Here again one cannot help wonder-
ing what the eight-year-old boy thought about all these
engagements and gatherings. He did obediently all that
he was told to do; a child still, he mastered all the difficulties as though they were a game.

The elegant Baron
von Grimm

He also found time and energy to go on composing.
But, surprisingly enough, it was less the French music
which attracted his attention than the work of certain
German musicians. The most gifted of them, Johann Schobert of Silesia, an
apostle of the new music, awoke uneasiness and opposition in Leopold Mozart.
But his son was caught and interested by his new, strongly expressive music.
It moved his innermost feelings as no sounds he had yet heard had ever done.
For the first time his artistic personality disagreed, however unconsciously,

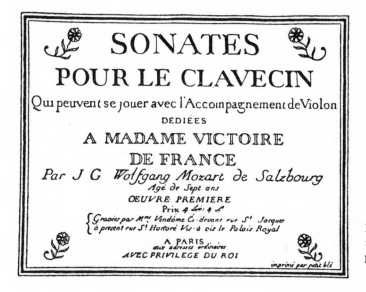

Mozart was seven when his
first work was
printed and published

The scholar Barrington attempted
to trace the source of the child
prodigy's powers

Johann Christian Bach acted as
Mozart's mentor and had a decisive
effect on his artistic career

London in the eighteenth century, when the
Mozarts visited it. Painting by Canaletto

with that of his father. It was far from Leopold's intentions that the tour
should have produced results of this kind.

But the significance of Paris was nothing compared with that of London.
For here Mozart was introduced to a new and unfamiliar world by which he
was at once captivated and which would continue to hold him in thrall: the
world of Handel, whose amanuensis, Smith, was still alive, and of the Italian
opera. But, more important still, it embraced the circle of Bach's pupils, including Karl Friedrich Abel and Johann Christian Bach, the great composer's
youngest son. Without in any way minimizing Leopold Mozart's importance,
it is fair to say it was from the 'London Bach' that Mozart learned most.

The visit produced results almost immediately. In Chelsea, where Leopold
Mozart stayed while recuperating from a throat disease, his son compiled the

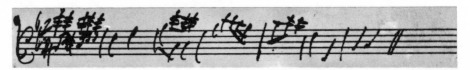

Mozart's unsteady handwriting

'London Sketchbook', a medley of various bits and pieces, sketches and notes. It is particularly of value, however, in that it contains thoughts written down without his father's supervision. Much of it is trivial stuff. But for this very reason it bears witness to an independent artistic will.

Daines Barrington, the English lawyer and naturalist (1727—1800), attempted to penetrate the 'mystery' of the child prodigy. He arranged systematic 'tests' whose results he later published in a scientific journal.

The situation had become critical. For the boy's understanding was beginning to develop and it was leading to a quiet resistance on his part. His own individual personality began to show itself. Until then he had looked on everything as merely a game and taken part in performances and entertainments without putting up any opposition, but now he began to distinguish

when eight years old

The 'child prodigies' played
to Londoners in this inn

between play and work — as Barrington observed. From now on he even showed a certain defiance when he had to stop amusing himself in his own way and demonstrate his artistry on the piano.

It was soon 1765. Opus 3, the sonatas for the English queen, were published; they were his first piano sonatas for four hands and an outcome of his duet-playing with Nannerl. A small madrigal (now in the British Museum) had also been published, as well as the first arias — only one is still extant — which began Mozart's association, later to become so important to him, with Italian operatic music. All these amount to no small achievement. Mozart's artistic personality had passed beyond the stage of merely reproducing others' creations.

Leopold Mozart was forced to admit that he had not given his son's ever-enquiring mind all that it needed. It is greatly to his credit, as a wise educator, that he immediately set about repairing the omissions as soon as the family returned from its journey.

This same outlook, however, was in tragic contrast to the shameful exhibitionism into which Leopold had been tempted in London. After the Mozarts' outstanding successes at Court and with knowledgeable audiences there was a certain withdrawal of general interest. To combat this, Leopold Mozart decided on a desperate step and arranged to present his children as 'spectacles'. He was completely aware of the risk and attempted to shift the blame for his unconcealed anger on to others, calling London a 'dangerous town' and finally taking flight altogether. The original cause of all this was a concert in the Swan Inn in Cornhill, about which the notice in the *Public Advertiser* gives full information. It attracted very small audiences. Nevertheless, Leopold announced daily performances in which, to cover the costs, the arts of the prodigy were presented in the manner of circus acts.

It appears that by now a shadow had fallen over the tour which had begun with such high hopes. Leopold Mozart hesitated as to his further plans. Originally they were to have returned home via Milan and Venice, but the invitation of Princess Caroline of Nassau-Weilburg attracted them to The Hague. After this Leopold was almost in despair when, while they were impatiently awaited in Salzburg, he and his son fell ill at Lille. They only reached the Dutch capital four weeks later, after travelling through Ghent, Antwerp and Rotterdam. 'I am in hopes that all will now go well,' wrote Leopold encouragingly, but it turned out differently. All their plans were ruined by a serious illness which confined Nannerl to her bed; for a time it was feared that she would die. Then after her miraculous recovery, a severe fever attacked Wolfgang Amadeus. Leopold's depression was only dissipated by the success, first, of their concerts in Amsterdam and The Hague and, second, of the Dutch edition of his own violin manual. Moreover, the weeks in bed were not completely lost, for the sick 'little composer' industriously and with great skill and charm committed to paper what he had absorbed during the journey.

'It would take too long,' explained Leopold Mozart, 'to describe our journey from Holland, through Amsterdam, over the Maas and then across

In a London press-notice Mozart
was advertised as
the greatest wonder of Europe

In Mozart's day the intellectual life
of Geneva was ruled
over by Voltaire and Rousseau

'It can be foretold that he will one
day be one of the greatest masters of
his art,' prophesied Dr Tissot
of the then-year-old Mozart

the bay near Mordyck to Antwerp.' They stopped at Malines, Brussels and
Valenciennes during this journey, which took them back to Paris after two
years on the road. They stayed in the city a full month, but nothing was the
same as during the first visit. The early enthusiasm, it appears, had worn off.
The child prodigies had become — according to Grimm — young persons,
who were no longer exciting enough to cause a sensation and who were therefore viewed in a more temperate manner. Some applause could still be stimulated by competitions on the organ or piano, and Mozart managed to write
the Kyrie for a *Messe à Paris* during some of his leisure time in the city. But
taken all in all their achievements during this second stay in the town where
they had had their first great triumphs remained far below their expectations.

Downcast, the Mozarts left for Dijon, where they were to play before the
Prince de Conti 'who has engaged us on account of the meeting of the States
of Burgundy', and to Lyon, with the general aim of going to Switzerland.

But even then the rest of the journey was unplanned.

When they arrived in Geneva they found the town in a tumult. Leopold
Mozart wrote of a 'civil war in full flame'. Voltaire, who lived in nearby
Ferney, spoke ironically of the conflict as the 'plaisanterie de Genève'. The
tumultuous quarrels between the citizens and nobility were really neither
more nor less than a foreboding of future dramatic events. The personality
of Rousseau was, of course, behind all these happenings. Amazingly, Leopold
Mozart, the Austrian Deputy Conductor, took no offence at all these new

ideas, not even those propagated by the atheist republicans, which were in direct opposition to his own religious principles and habits. Presumably the Mozarts played before the members of the commission who had come to Geneva from Berne and Zürich to settle the dispute. On the other hand, the family purposely avoided Voltaire and, half afraid, half antagonistic, refused to visit Ferney, although the sick old man very much wanted to hear the 'petit Mazar' (as he wrote to Madame d'Epinay in Paris), the 'phenomenon sparkling on the gloomy horizon of Geneva'. But the godless 'archrogue', as the Mozart family christened the great satirist, had to go without seeing this 'miracle in the flesh'.

In Lausanne the nobility showed a certain interest, particularly Prince Ludwig of Württemberg, for whom Mozart wrote various pieces for the flute which are unfortunately no longer extant. All this was carefully noted down by Leopold Mozart. On the other hand he never mentions the name of Dr Auguste Tissot in his letters any more than he had mentioned the learned Daines Barrington, although in his carefully observed analysis of the 'jeune Mozart' the Swiss doctor also bestowed suitable praise on his father. Tissot, who as a doctor and psychologist became interested in the Mozart phenomenon, was the first to consider the ten-year-old boy not as a sensation but as a human personality. In a review called *Aristide* he made the following prophecy: 'It can be foretold with some certainty that he will one day be one of the greatest masters of his art.'

Nothing is known of the Mozarts' activities in Berne. They took the opportunity of becoming 'acquainted with scholars'. Did these, perhaps, include Albrecht von Haller, the doctor-author, or Vinzenz Bernhard von Tscharner, a disciple of Klopstock? After all the hurry and agitation, excitement and applause of the past two years' tour Mozart benefited from this period of peace and normal life. Hardly anything was said about creative work but, although Leopold Mozart's letters from Switzerland contain little more than accounts, notes and dates, nevertheless every line breathes a certain relief and peaceful well-being.

Before setting out for home via Winterthur and Schaffhausen the Mozarts spent a pleasant and eventful period in Zürich. Their private engagements were apparently more important than their public successes, such as the concerts they gave for the 'Musik-Gesellschaft' (Music Society), for they took the Mozarts into the heart of the town's active cultural life which at this particular time was attracting the attention of all Germany, if not of all Europe.

Zürich had many illustrious inhabitants. Bodmer and Breitinger, fathers of the new literature which had formed a link between north and south, were still alive. The spirit which animated them was not only reflected in men like Klopstock and the young Lessing; in their own town they could see growing up around them literary and artistic powers striving towards a new era or, as they would have put it, a new paradise. There were men like Johann Georg Sulzer, for instance, or Pestalozzi, or Lavater, or the painter Fuseli. The uncontested leader of this company of zealous thinkers was the charming Solomon Gessner, publisher, printer and bookseller, painter and poet,

Salomon Gessner who acted as host to the Mozarts in Zürich

who took an active part in the town's affairs. His hospitable house, 'The Swan', was the centre of Zürich's intellectual and social life and the goal of all who came to the town, including famous personalities like Ewald von Kleist, Wieland, Goethe and Anton Graaff, who painted a portrait of Gessner in 'The Swan'. After Gessner's marriage to the beautiful Judith Heidegger, the so-called 'Tuesday gathering', a friendly meeting held in Gessner's house, developed into a regular society whose ideas and activities assorted well with the classically decorated rooms of the house. Gessner welcomed the Salzburg party with open arms. It was an unforgettable experience for both him and Leopold Mozart to see, hear and converse with each other. The latter wrote that Solomon Gessner and his brother Johann, an associate of the physicist Albrecht von Haller, made 'their visit very pleasant', and their parting 'most sorrowful'. Not only were the Mozarts guests of the Gessner circle on 3rd October 1766 (Mozart noted the date); the poet also rewarded the children for their playing with a copy of the latest edition of his works.

This encounter with the ideas of the new age was certainly as important to Mozart's intellectual development as his meeting with Bach's son was to his musical progress. He completely forgot Melchior Grimm (who incidentally was the only one of all the boy's spectators to express a fear lest the 'quickly ripe fruit shall fall too soon'), unlike his father, for whom the brilliant *encyclopédiste* embodied all the greatness of the age.

The rest of the journey after Zürich was an anticlimax. It was not until they reached Donaueschingen that they enjoyed the splendour of Court favour once again. Encouraged, the Mozarts travelled through Ulm, Günzburg

Michael, brother of Joseph Haydn

Dr Sylvester Barisani

The ten-year-old 'Wolfgang Mozart' named,
as of right, amongst the great of Salzburg

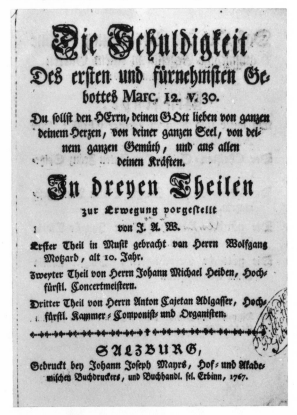

Die Schuldigkeit
Des ersten und fürnehmisten Gebottes Marc. 12. v. 30.
Du sollst den HErrn, deinen GOtt lieben von ganzem
deinem Herzen, von deiner ganzen Seel, von deinem ganzen Gemüth, und aus allen
deinen Kräften.

In dreyen Theilen
zur Erwegung vorgestellt
von J. A. W.

Erster Theil in Musik gebracht von Herrn Wolfgang
Mozard, alt 10. Jahr.

Zweyter Theil von Herrn Johann Michael Heiden, Hochfürstl. Concertmeistern.

Dritter Theil von Herrn Anton Cajetan Adlgasser, Hochfürstl. Kammer-Componist und Organisten.

SALZBURG,
Gedruckt bey Johann Joseph Mayrs, Hof- und Akade-
mischen Buchdruckers, und Buchhandl. sel. Erbinn, 1767.

and Dillingen, where they were the prince's guests, to Markt Biberach. There the Count of Babenhausen, a member of the Fugger family, invited the ten-year-old Wolfgang to take part in a contest in organ-playing with a twelve-year-old boy called Bachmann. Finally, on 30th November 1766, the coach containing the family arrived back home at the house in Salzburg.

Between their departure and return lay three crucial years. The child prodigy had developed an independent personality and his sister had grown into a young lady. The tour had impressed on Leopold Mozart exactly what task his children imposed on him. 'Every moment I lose is lost for ever, and I know now, if ever I have done, how precious time is

Vienna in the eighteenth century, seen from the Belvedere

for young people.' A notebook for counterpoint practice shows his eagerness to broaden his son's musical education. The recognition accorded to the family by the Salzburg Court (which, incidentally, noted their absence in England in the Court diary) resulted in commissions for compositions. Side by side with the respected composer Michael Haydn, who had held a post in Salzburg since 1762, and Cajetan Adlgasser, the ten-year-old Wolfgang was invited to contribute to the oratorio *Die Schuldigkeit des ersten und fürnehmsten Gebottes* ('The obligation of the first and greatest commandment') by Ignaz Anton Weiser. He also wrote the Funeral Cantata for Lent and turned various pieces that he had heard during the journey into concert studies. But, most important of all, he wrote his first work for the stage, the Latin comedy *Apollo et Hyacinth,* for the University Theatre.

Leopold Mozart hoped, and was convinced, that Vienna would offer the best opportunity for opera and operetta. Less than a year after the Mozarts had returned home they set off again, but the high hopes with which the family approached Vienna in the autumn of 1767, prepared to add new and greater triumphs to their past conquests in the city, were soon quenched. The spreading smallpox epidemic forced Leopold to leave the capital with his wife and children and seek refuge in the house of Count Podstatsky, a dean of the cathedral, at Olmütz. But fate overtook them. It is true that the serious illness, whose scars remained visible on Wolfgang Amadeus in particular to the end of his life, enforced on him a period of leisure of which he had long stood in need, but the unfortunate start of the Vienna tour proved to be typical of the further course of events.

Disillusionment   One has to go back to Mozart's childhood, and perhaps this period in particular, to understand the polarity of his character and fate. Mozart, a small man, was not handsome, at least not as ideally handsome as one would like to imagine him. His delicate constitution, aggravated by continued physical hardship, gave his face a 'sallow colour', as his sister put it, a certain pallor. Although always ready for gaiety and practical jokes, he was sometimes given to depression and 'bad temper', a formula which often occurs in his later letters. The fact that his lust for life was accompanied by a touching faith in the kindliness of death was not only a result of his religious and philosophic opinions (particularly after he had read Mendelssohn's *Phaidon)* but a typical part of his nature. Only this can explain how he could write, with equal conviction, *Don Giovanni* as well as *The Magic Flute, Eine Kleine Nachtmusik,* as well as the *Ave Verum.*

All the causes of Mozart's early death and his ability to make months do the work of years can be discerned in the history of his childhood. It is doubtful whether, when at Olmütz, passing the time by doing card tricks, he was still naive, still child enough, to escape harm being done to his constitution and his psyche. He, as one who had the pox, was greeted on his arrival in Vienna with alarm, and when, on top of this, the expected triumphal entry was not forthcoming, he must have been crushed with disappointment.

Leopold Mozart was even more disappointed. It is true that they were received at Court, charmingly entertained by the Emperor Joseph and given motherly praise by Maria Theresa, but Leopold's plan to obtain recognition for the art of his now 'mature' children did not succeed. The favour of the Viennese nobility was not a satisfactory substitute. Everywhere he scented envy, professional jealousy and malice, which caused him to say hard words about Vienna and the Viennese.

But at last the moment of success seemed to have arrived. The Emperor desired Mozart to write an Italian opera buffa, his first opera, the musical direction of which, so ran the commission, was to be in the hands of the twelve-year-old boy himself.

It would indeed have been amazing if *La Finta Semplice* (written to a libretto by Marco Cottellini) had actually been produced in Vienna, the city whose musical life was ruled over by Christoph Willibald Gluck and Pietro

Doubts have recently been cast on the authenticity of this famous picture by Helbling
since in it Mozart's eyes are brown instead of blue, as they were in reality

Christoph Willibald Gluck

Pietro Metastasio, the librettist

Metastasio. In the event a tissue of intrigues, behind which Leopold unjustly suspected Gluck's hand, bedevilled the undertaking from the start. Easter 1768, when the first performance was to have taken place, passed by. Autumn came. Neither anger nor complaints nor even a protest to the Emperor himself, succeeded in obtaining a performance. 'Thus one fights one's way through life', said Leopold resignedly. 'If a man has no talent he is unhappy enough; but if he has talent he is pursued by envy in proportion to his skill.'

Worse than the financial distress brought on by the long waiting, which drove Leopold into debt, much against the grain of his character, was the feeling of artistic failure which wounded his pride and honour. (The fact that the Goldoni-Wie opera was performed in Salzburg at the command of the Prince Bishop in 1769 was only a small consolation.)

But the stay in Vienna was not completely fruitless. If Leopold's twelve-year-old son lacked the maturity for full-scale opera, at least he had tried his strength and suitability for every sphere of his art. His second attempt at

The twelve-year-old Mozart was allowed to present himself to the Emperor in the Waisenhauskirche, Vienna

writing for the theatre — later to be his particular speciality — was better suited to his age and creative powers.

At the invitation of Franz Anton Mesmer, the doctor whose magnetism-therapy was a sensation of the day, Mozart wrote the music for *Bastien et Bastienne*, a one-act play by Wilhelm Weiskern, after Rousseau. The little musical play charmed the company of guests who saw it at Mesmer's private theatre in his house in the main road. It gave the Mozart family a considerable amount of gratification though they were even better pleased when Wolfgang was permitted to conduct his Festival Mass in the Waisenhauskirche in the Rennweg.

Indeed, in many ways the Vienna tour, from which the Mozarts returned to Salzburg at the beginning of January 1769, was important. First it was important from the artistic point of view, despite the commercial fiasco, in that it started Mozart on the two kinds of music with which he was to lead his age and, indeed, the ages to come. Compared with the orchestral works of these months, in which his feeling for style, his taste and his gradual dissociation from Johann Christian Bach already reveal an individual personality, the two dramatic works are only first attempts. But as such they meant that Mozart had advanced a step towards the ultimate goal.

Leopold Mozart gradually became convinced in Vienna that this first trial of strength and human endurance would only be of value as a prelude, a preparation for the later achievement of his long-formed plan. Only in Italy, the native land of opera, he believed, could he expect complete success. 'Why should I stay put in Salzburg, sighing and hoping vainly for a stroke of luck, seeing Wolfgang grow up while I and my children are led by the nose, until I reach an age when I can no longer bear long journeys and Wolfgang's age is such as to rob him of all interest? Why should my son take his first step in vain, thanks to the Vienna opera, and not even attempt to pursue the path so clearly indicated for him?'

This acute thinking, in which resentment was mixed with clear-sightedness, led Leopold Mozart to make the necessary preparations in Vienna for a tour in Italy. Johann Adolph Hasse, a seventy-year-old opera-composer, had put the boy through

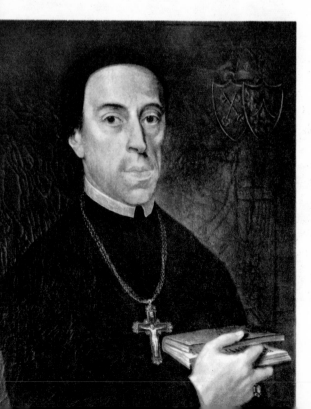

The Hagenauers' son Pater Dominicus, to whom the Dominicus Mass was dedicated, was a great friend of the young Mozart, who wept bitterly when he entered a monastery

a thorough examination and given his 'gifted, sensitive and cultured' father a letter of recommendation to the Italian musical world. This document contains the greatest praise and admiration of Wolfgang Amadeus who, it runs, performed everything 'so prettily that one cannot help being fond of him. One thing is certain: if his development keeps pace with his age he will become a marvel. Only his father must not over-indulge him or spoil him with excessive, exaggerated praise. This is the only danger that I fear for him.'

Once again, one wonders if the events, mounting inevitably to a crisis, made any impression on the person most concerned. With every step that Mozart took he learned something new. In Vienna it was operatic and orchestral music, while during a period of leisure in Salzburg commissions for music suited to the Court life of a spiritual princedom set him new problems. His attention was drawn to the more intricate style

Prince Bishop Sigismund von Schrattenbach

Schrattenbach contributed towards the cost of the Mozarts' journey to Italy out of his own purse

Italy in 1780:
the Mozarts, father
and son, travelled
all round the country
on three occasions

of chamber music, such as serenades and divertimenti, as well as liturgical and church music. Both types of music were to figure largely in his writings from that time onward.

In particular the form and expression of his religious thought as shown in his Masses tell us a good deal about Mozart. From his first Mass to his last, the incomplete Requiem written when he was dying, a straight line can be traced which is not only of interest from the formal and stylistic standpoints. The Dominicus Mass already shows promise; it was written by Mozart for his friend Dominicus Hagenauer, the son of the Mozarts' landlord, when he celebrated his first mass. Here, too, Viennese influences can still be seen.

Piece by piece the complete Mozart was built up. Now was the time to take a decisive step.

Thanks to the understanding and kindness of the Prince Bishop, Sigismund von Schrattenbach, who gave his unpaid concert-master the wherewithal for the Italian journey, Leopold was finally enabled to set off over the Alps with his son.

Having prepared themselves by reading all available books on Italy—Keyssler's travel book which they had studied served those left at home as a comforting substitute for taking part in the actual journey — the father and son once more entered the coach in December 1769. For the first time Wolfgang Amadeus wrote various letters of his own. From them it is clear that at bottom he was still a true child, enjoying the winter journey over the Brenner Pass as an adventure and amusement: 'My heart is absolutely filled with pure pleasure, because the journey is such fun and because it is so warm in the carriage and because our coachman is such a fine chap who goes jolly fast when the road allows. I think Papa has already described the journey to Mama ...'

Italian journey

Journeys to Italy were a common extravagance of northern, and especially German, artists and scholars of the eighteenth century: they formed one aspect of their enthusiasm for the classical age. Particularly since Winckelmann had set up the classical ideal for

The Mozarts looked up the memorable sights of the places they were going to in Johann Georg Keyssler's travel book

Johann Georg Keyßlers,
der Königlich Großbrittannischen Societät der Wissenschaften
Mitgliedes,

Neueste Reisen

durch
Deutschland, Böhmen, Ungarn, die Schweiz,
Italien und Lothringen,
worinnen der
Zustand und das Merkwürdigste dieser Länder
beschrieben,
und vermittelst der Natürlichen, Gelehrten und Politischen Geschichte,
der Mechanik, Maler-Bau- und Bildhauerkunst, Münzen und Alterthümer,
wie auch mit verschiedenen Kupfern
erläutert wird.

Neue und vermehrte Auflage,
welche
mit Zusätzen und mit einer Vorrede
von dem Leben des Verfassers
begleitet hat
M. Gottfried Schütze
Königlich Dänischer Consistorial-Assessor, des Pädagogii zu Altona Rector, der Königl. Preuß.
Akademie wie auch der Königl. Dänischen Societät der Wissenschaften Mitglied.

Mit Königl. Poln. und Churfürstl. Sächl. allergnädigster Freyheit.

Hannover, 1751.
Im Verlage sel. Nicolai Försters und Sohns Erben
Hof-Buchhandlung.

AMEDEO VOLFANGO MOZARTO SALISBVRGENSI
PVERO DVODENNI
ARTE MVSICA LAVDEM OMNEM FIDEMQ. PRAETERGRESSO
QO NOMINE GALLORVM ANGLORVMQ. REGIBVS CARO
PETRVS LVIATVS HOSPITI SVAVISSIMO
EFFIGIEM IN DOMESTICO ODEO P. C.
ANNO CIƆIƆCCLXX.

Mozart at fourteen

the eighteenth century, the great desire of those with pretensions to culture was to seek 'the country of the Greeks' in the culture of its Italian descendants, to seek it 'with the soul'.

As far as musicians were concerned, there had been other motives ever since the birth of opera at the beginning of the seventeenth century. The musicians' quest was less for the past than for the music of contemporary Italy. Just as Dürer's artistic outlook underwent a complete change when he came into contact with Raphael's work, so the musicians of the eighteenth century looked on Italian music as the supreme model. This adoption of the language and music of the south went far beyond pure imitation and became an abnegation of self, so that only a few were able to retain anything of their individuality. Even Johann Sebastian Bach, who never went to Italy, thought it imperative, a duty, to be intimately acquainted with Italian music and its peculiarities.

Italianism made German opera into yet another aesthetic province of Italy until Mozart's day and determined the atmosphere of Court music, just as French baroque writing dominated the literary sympathies of the Courts. To have been in Italy, to have had a success in Milan, Venice and Naples became proof of artistic quality. Both Handel and Gluck had begun their careers with the Italian style and it had led them to fame and fortune. The Italian *opera seria*, the opera which was a sequence of statuesque, florid arias loosely attached to a theme taken from Greek mythology, and the *opera buffa,* an effervescent, good-humoured entertainment closely related to the *commedia dell'arte,* between them conquered almost the whole of the European musical stage. And the matter they expressed was symptomatic of the philosophy and social ideas of the age.

Under these circumstances, it was clearly a necessity for Leopold Mozart to take his son to the source of fame with all possible haste. The Mozarts' three Italian journeys were certainly not pleasure trips. Even though one looks in vain in the travelling Mozarts' letters for allusions to 'classical' opinions and remarks about art, it is evident that Leopold intended to combine the musical aims of the journey with a little further education in general culture (they had of course 'read up' everything in Keyssler's book, so that there was no need to send reports home). But the real function of the journey was to introduce Mozart to the native opera of Italy and, by introducing him to the great men of the operatic empire, to set a triumphant seal on his years of study.

Wolfgang Amadeus did himself and his father credit when playing before both the general public and musical connoisseurs. Leopold's high hopes for

the Italian tour were already
fulfilled in the first stopping-
places — they were hailed with
enthusiasm in Innsbruck, exul-
tation in Rovereto and amazed
admiration in Verona. Both in
Rovereto and Verona crowds
packed into the church to hear
the young organist and the ex-
citement which his art aroused in the aristocratic circles of Verona's music-
lovers found expression in poetry and newspaper articles. Pietro Luggiati
who shared the generally expressed wish 'to see him painted on canvas after
nature in order to preserve a permanent memento of him', commissioned a
portrait of the '*raro e portentoso giovane*'. The fact that Mozart was no longer
a 'child prodigy' but an artist who deserved to be taken seriously for the sake
of his artistry rather than of his youth, made this tour completely different
from all the previous ones.

This 'Italian journey' was to be the same crucial turning point in Mozart's
life and development that a similar journey was to Goethe at a later age. It
was salutary for Mozart to hear and study Italian opera on the spot — which
he did as soon as they reached Verona, Mantua and Cremona. He could
observe, absorb and judge from the living model. Those around him were
amazed to see how effortlessly he adapted himself to the new atmosphere.

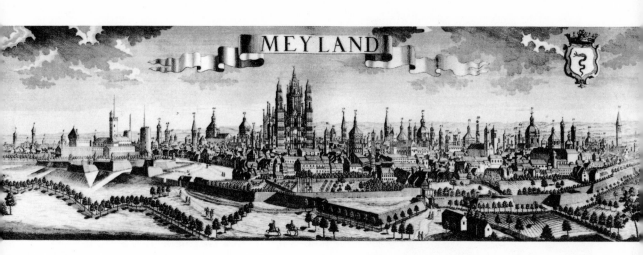

Despite the bitter cold from which they suffered while travelling and in their unheated lodgings, both Mozarts were in good spirits. And they were even more cheerful when they found comfortable quarters with the Augustines in Milan and were able to take part in the lively activities of the town's academies and societies.

They even sampled the carnival. Leopold Mozart, by nature a thrifty man, summoned a tailor, had 'coats' and 'bayoutes' (hats) made and was charmed by his son's costume, though less charmed by the 'foolery' to which he was asked to lend himself at his advanced age.

Their chief patron in Milan, Carl Joseph von Firmian, paved the way for them with benevolence and understanding. In the capital of Lombardy, as everywhere in Italy, they met with the customs which had been native to the culture of the Italian Courts since the time of the Renaissance. The same 'academies' to which Corelli, Handel and Winckelmann owed their fame hastened to acclaim the budding genius of the 14-year-old boy, with true humanistic breadth of view, discreet encouragement and, at the same time, the enthusiasm of the connoisseur.

The concerts and demonstrations which he gave before music specialists and cultured dilettantes were no longer 'sensations' but convincing proofs of his capabilities which were received with just appreciation. Amongst other reliable spectators, there were Nicola Piccini, a fertile opera composer, whose authority was set up in opposition to Gluck's by his contemporaries, and Giovanni Battista Sammartini, who has an important place in the history of

Joseph Mysliweczek

instrumental music.

As yet Mozart had still not written any operas for Italy. He was still only an extremely attentive observer of all that he could learn about opera from Hasse and Piccini in their Italian setting. He gave the first proof of his ability when he was commissioned to write an aria for Metastasio's *Demofoonte*. It was immediately obvious that he already had more to say than the established masters whom he took as his models. On 13th March 1770 Leopold Mozart informed the family at Salzburg that he had received his first commission for an opera in Milan.

This commission, or *serittura*, meant that Mozart had joined the ranks of Italian opera composers. And since the first performance of the opera *Mitridate, Rè di Ponte* ('Mithridates, King of Pontus') would not take place until Christmas, the Mozarts could continue their journey in the meantime. The opera was written to a libretto by Cigna-Santi, of Turin, after the tragedy of the same name by Racine. While they were in Lodi, the town associated with Barbarossa, Mozart composed his first string quartet 'in the evening at the inn', showing that he was already interested in the noblest form of chamber music. Although in Germany the quartet, as a form, had passed through its experimental stages and had been crystallized for ever by Haydn, it was not until now that Mozart was moved or excited by it — to be precise, by Sammartini's 'concertini'. That he became profoundly interested in the problems peculiar to chamber music can be seen from the many quartets he later wrote 'out of boredom'.

There is something overwhelming about the constant zeal with which Mozart strove to absorb everything worth learning and remembering, despite the counter-attractions of various activities more suited to his childish high spirits. This apparent contradiction, visible from his earliest years, was a distinguishing feature of his character. It is shown particularly clearly in his experiences in Italy, the sympathy with which he was received and the spontaneous response he gave to all this encouragement during the months he spent in the country. It was not only praise and appreciation which drew forth this response from him, but above all the serious interest which people took in him.

Padre Martini

Count Giovanni Pallavicini-Centurioni extended his patronage to the Mozarts and invited the most distinguished members of Bologna society to meet them in his house. 'What gives me particular pleasure,' wrote Leopold Mozart to his wife, 'is that we are extraordinarily popular here and that Wolfgang is more admired than in any other Italian city, for this is the home of many masters, artists and learned men. It is here, too, that he has been the most thoroughly tested, and this increases his fame throughout Italy, for P. Martini is the idol of Italy and he speaks of Wolfgang with such admiration after having put him through all manner of examinations.' Giovanni Battista Martini, the 'Padre Martini', who is known to musicology as a theoretician and teacher of the first rank, worked for his 'noble Chevalier Mozart' with the greatest self-sacrifice and kindness. He taught and examined him in the difficult arts of counterpoint and the canonic rules of the Palestrina school. Thus Padre Martini may also be called one of Mozart's teachers. His kindness and that of 'Boemo', the Czech composer Johann Mysliweczek, whom they met during their second stay in Bologna, made the memory of the tour particularly agreeable to the Mozarts.

Mozart's writing in 1770

These meetings, arranged by Pallavicini, had a symbolic significance in Mozart's development, for the circle of people who took a fervent interest in the boy was chiefly composed of men who were reaching the end of their careers, who embodied the brilliance of former ages. With the exception of Martini who, as head of the Bologna school, possessed an aura of infallibility in the musical life of Europe, the rest had already passed the zenith of their fame. But their names still retained a great deal of their erstwhile glamour and represented the cream of the exponents of the old traditional Italian opera.

The Mozarts also met the castrati Giuseppe Aprile and Carlo Broschi-Farinelli, the 'ragazzo' Farinelli who had lent his support to the opera-faction opposing Handel in London and who now, after a life richly filled with art and intrigues in Spain, was ending his days in a palace outside the gates of Bologna, in an aura of wealth and fame.

When the Mozarts left Bologna — at the end of March 1770 — they were eager to reach Rome as soon as possible. During a short stay in Florence they became acquainted with the violinist Pietro Nardini and the *noblissime dilettante*, Eugenio Ligneville, who 'is the best contrapuntist in all Italy and has accordingly given Wolfgang the most difficult fugues with the most difficult themes to work out; but Wolfgang developed and played them with no more trouble than if he were eating a piece of bread.' Although not easily roused, Leopold Mozart reached the point of enthusiasm. 'I wished that you yourself could see Florence and the whole area and position of this town,' he wrote to his wife. 'You would agree that this is the place to live and die. In these few days I shall see everything that there is to be seen.'

They were endeared still further to Florence by the fact that they again saw the singer Giovanni Manzuoli whom they had first met in London. Wolfgang formed a friendship with Thomas Linley, an English boy violinist of his own age whom he had met in the house of the poetess Corilla, and was sorry to have to part from him so swiftly. And their spirits were not raised by a five-day journey through streaming rain. Leopold Mozart was peevish. 'I will not give you a long description of this abominable journey; just imagine a countryside mostly without buildings and with the most abominable inns, filth, nothing to eat, except sometimes, with luck, eggs or broccoli . . .'

Nevertheless, Rome in all the glory and magnificence of her Easter celebrations soon captivated them. With a good deal of skill and worldly-wise humour, Leopold Mozart launched himself and his son into all the festivities.

The Mozarts entered Rome through the Piazza del Popolo

They retained their convenient incognito and were highly amused at the mistake when the crowd and the Swiss Guard took them for a prince and his tutor, because they spoke German and wore fine clothing.

A similar episode occurred when they were about to be received by the Secretary of State, Cardinal Pallavicini. Leopold Mozart gives a description: 'Then it happened that Wolfgang was standing between the chairs of two cardinals, one of whom was Cardinal Pallavicini. He beckoned to Wolfgang and said: "Will you be so kind as to tell me, in confidence, who you are?" Wolfgang told him all about himself. The cardinal answered him with the greatest astonishment: "Oh, are you the famous boy about whom they have told me so much?" And Wolfgang asked: "Are you not Cardinal Pallavicini?" The Cardinal answered: "Yes, I am he. Why?" Then Wolfgang told him that

'Today Vesuvius smoked a lot . . .' was Mozart's
laconic description of Naples' outstanding feature. He was more interested
in the 'Molo' (a famous promenade), music and the theatre

we had letters for His Holiness and were to be received in audience. The
cardinal showed great pleasure at this, remarked that Wolfgang spoke good
Italian, and amongst other things said: "I can also speak a leetle-a German,"
etc. When we left Wolfgang kissed his hand and the cardinal lifted his biretta
and made him a polite bow.'

This scherzo interlude in the gay, grandiose atmosphere of the Eternal City
brought back the pleasant feelings which had dominated the journey as far
as Florence. They divided their time between visits to the palaces of the
nobility, such as, say, those of the Chigis or the Althems, and concerts at
the houses of the aristocracy. Wolfgang felt in such a good humour that
he found the time to write a 'contredance' for his sister and to add his own
playful marginal comments out of *Roma Caput Mundi* to his father's letters.

Like Florence, Rome appealed greatly to Leopold Mozart. It was only the
onset of the summer heat that reconciled him to leaving the basin of the Tiber
surrounded by its stifling hills and travelling on to Capua and Naples. Naples,
the pinnacle of the Italian opera of the day, pleased him most on account of

its situation and historical buildings. But it also annoyed him because of the general tendency of all its people, even 'people of distinction', to superstition. His son was interested in other aspects of the city. 'Today Vesuvius smoked a lot.' This is the only allusion to the city's outstanding feature. With a certain lack of respect, he wrote of King Ferdinand IV of Naples that 'he always stands on a footstool at the opera so that he looks as though he is a bit taller than the Queen.' But the most interesting part of the expedition was its artistic side. There were many concerts for the nobility, as for instance for the English ambassador, Sir William Hamilton, renowned for his archaeological knowledge (and for the exploits of his second wife, Emma). In the foreground, of course, was the theatre. Once again they met Jommelli who was just at this time suffering a pitiable failure with his latest operatic work. And they made the acquaintance of Giovanni Paesiello, Francesco Majo and other leading figures of the Neapolitan operatic world. Mozart might have had the honour of becoming one of them. For, as in Bologna and Rome, he was

In the Sistine Chapel Mozart heard Allegri's Miserere

Clemens P. P. XIV.

invited to accept a *scrittura* from the city.

In Rome, however, they were to be greeted by greater surprises than even Naples could offer. Wolfgang Amadeus was to be distinguished by a mark of the highest honour.

In Naples, Leopold Mozart had reassured his wife in an amused letter about an account which he had sent her concerning one of his son's escapades in Rome. This was the famous episode that took place in the Sistine Chapel on Ash Wednesday, when Gregorio Allegri's *Miserere* was traditionally sung; it was forbidden on pain of excommunication to copy this rather complex contrapuntal work; but Mozart, after hearing it once, wrote it down from memory. His mother immediately had visions of him outlawed and excommunicated. But soon Leopold was able to soothe her fears: 'There is nothing to fear: on the contrary, it did him great credit.'

Only a few days after their return to Rome, they noticed that Cardinal Pallavicini was addressing Wolfgang as 'Signor Cavaliere'. On 5th July they learned from Pallavicini that what they had taken for a joke was in fact

Leopold Mozart copied the diploma which the Pope awarded his son for Padre Martini

Pope Clement XIV

serious: the Cardinal bestowed on Mozart the cross and diploma of the Order of the Golden Spur which Clement XIV had conferred on him: three days later they were received in audience by the Pope himself.

This unusual distinction, particularly for a 14-year-old boy, led to various developments. Possession of the Order gave Mozart the right to call himself *Cavaliere dello speron d'oro* (Knight of the Golden Spur) and also pledged him always to bear the Order '*juxta modum et formam*' ('as prescribed'). But although Gluck and Ditters von Dittersdorf are sometimes known by their titles, Mozart is almost never associated with his. Only one or two examples can be found: the occasion of a scandal which took place in Augsburg; Leopold's letters to his son during the latter's journey to Paris in 1778, which were addressed to Chevalier Mozart at first though the title suddenly ceased to be used; and on a Viennese programme at a time when Mozart had definitely decided to break with Salzburg.

Mozart the Knight

Was it modesty which caused him to suppress a title which had once been borne by Orlando di Lasso, which came from the Vatican, indeed from the Pope himself, and was therefore even more distinguished than the titles

Charles Burney

conferred on Gluck, Dittersdorf and Vogler? Why did his father, in general so proud of Wolfgang, not broadcast his delight to all and sundry as he usually did about his smallest successes, not least with the intention of bringing it to the ears of Salzburg gossip, and above all the Residency? About this honour not a word was spoken. Only the remark that he was amused when he 'heard himself being called Signor Cavaliere all the time'. There must have been special reasons for this reticence and everything suggests that the Mozarts feared to anger the Knights Ruperti of Salzburg who would certainly not have been pleased if their conductor's son, an 'inferior', who sat at the servants' table in the bishop's palace, were to put himself on the same level as them.

For the first time, the inoffensive life of the inoffensive Mozart was involved in the social strife which continued to infuriate him at intervals until his death. As yet he did not find it insulting to be 'forcibly held back'. But it was not long before he began to be annoyed. For however much he appeared to belittle his knightly dignity, calling himself 'Knight of the Golden Spur and, as soon as I marry, of the two horns', he was sensitive where his honour was concerned. And quite apart from this, many more doors would have been open to him as a knight than as plain Wolfgang Amadeus Mozart. But in itself it meant little to him. It is probable that when he was in Paris in 1778 the golden Order went the same way as his mother's golden watch — to the pawnshop.

After this distinction in Rome, Mozart was again honoured in Bologna, to which he went back in the autumn of the same year. Through Martini's good offices he was accepted, on the strength of the examination composition he had done, as a *compositore* in the highly respected Accademia Filarmonica. Among those who saw Mozart at this time was the English traveller and musicologist, Dr Charles Burney, Fanny Burney's father. He later wrote that he well remembered the little German whose precocious and extraordinary talents had astonished London a few years before, and that since his arrival in Italy he had been much admired in Naples and Rome. Mozart himself left it to others to recount these triumphs. He was preoccupied at this time by his exertions for the Milan opera. The first performance was to take place in December. As Leopold was involved in an accident on the road between Naples and Rome and fell ill with rheumatism, they went directly from Bologna to Milan without stopping at Genoa as they had intended.

The journey through northern Italy was 'uncomfortable' and rainy. It was now October.

A certain unrest, an understandable nervousness and anxiety, overtook the aspirant to fame in Italian opera. Again and again his postscripts to his father's letters home contain the plea to his mother and sister to pray 'that the opera goes well'. This period of suspense and tension was filled with writing, walking, sleeping and ever more writing. But from the very first rehearsals it was clear that the singers were pleased, which meant that he had crossed the first hurdle. Musicians hastened to give their praises — Giovanni Battista

The Teatro Ducale in Milan, where *Mitridate* received its first performance

Lampugnani, Sammartini, the orchestral players. And Leopold Mozart himself, the most critical of all, opined without any partisan feeling that 'he [Wolfgang] has written the opera well and with much spirit'.

It seemed that nothing could now stand in the way of success. 'It is now entirely up to the whims of the public,' wrote Leopold to his wife. 'Apart from a few crumbs of praise, we have not really much to lose. In this strange world of ours we have already embarked on many enterprises and God has always been with us. Now we stand on the brink of this undertaking, a fairly weighty one on many accounts, and God will still be with us. On St Stephen's Day, an hour after Ave Maria, you may think of Maestro Don Amadeo at the keyboard in the orchestra and myself as a spectator in a box amongst the audience . . .'

When St Stephen's Day 1770, 20th December, came it made up for all the care and anxiety of the previous period. The packed Teatro Ducale rang with cheers and cries of 'Evviva il maestro! Evviva il maestrino!' And with each of the following performances — there were twenty in all — the enthusiasm increased. 'Our son's opera continues to receive universal applause and is, as the Italians says, *alle stelle*,' wrote Leopold proudly to Anna Maria.

Mozart had conquered his world, the theatre. After the Milan success the rest of the journey was spent in pure enjoyment; there was a pleasure trip to Turin, a carnival in Venice, music-making in Padua, where Mozart received a commission for an *azione teatrale*, *La Betulia Liberata*, relaxation in Vicenza and a pleasant return to Verona. There, in March 1771, they found a new commission for Milan, to write the festival music for the marriage of Archduke Ferdinand, which was to take place in the autumn.

By the time they returned to Salzburg Mozart was fifteen years old. Leopold had decided while they were still in Verona that they must take larger lodgings: 'We can no longer sleep all together (like soldiers): Wolfgang is no longer a boy of seven.' But in fact it was not until 1773 that the Mozarts moved to the spacious first floor of a house belonging to a dancing master and situated near the Hannibalgarten.

There is little to be told about the few months of 1771 which the Mozarts spent at home in Salzburg. Normal life resumed its course. The fame of the young 'knight' who could not use the title, was put firmly in its place — across the border in Italy. A report in the *Vossische Zeitung* of Berlin, speaking of events in Milan and Venice, praised Mozart's 'genial modesty which gives added value to his precocious powers' and was of the opinion that the praise must 'give extreme pleasure to his father who travels with him'.

Leopold Mozart, who did indeed experience this pleasure, was able to

The stone steps leading up to the dancing master's house where the Mozarts lived in Salzburg

For the wedding of the young
Archduke Ferdinand, Mozart composed his
'azione teatrale' on the theme of the marriage of
Ascanius to the nymph Silvia

find confirmation of the efficacy of his theories of education and upbringing in the success of this tour. After sharing all their troubles and joys, the father and son had become true friends and companions. And the father had come to believe (or hope) that this happy situation would never change. It is a pity that Leopold Mozart never wrote the biography of his son which he proposed in the second edition of his violin manual. Wolfgang Amadeus, who seemed incapable of being spoiled by triumphs, had gained a new self-confidence during the tour in Italy. He had tried and proved his powers. He had won not only a position for himself as an artist before the public but an independent artistic standpoint as a composer. Out of his experience of the world, he had moulded a personal and professional character. Although he was still child enough to enjoy the stories from the *Arabian Nights* (he read them in Italian) his other reading gave signs that he was coming to intellectual maturity. For instance, he read *Télèmaque,* the picaresque novel written for the young Dauphin by Fénélon, the French seventeenth-century mystic, pedagogue and forerunner of Rousseau; and it soon became clear from the opinions he expressed that he had read with a receptive mind. Meanwhile he used the 'rest' period in Salzburg to write the music for the dramatic oratorio *La Betulia.* But they were still waiting impatiently for Guiseppe Paini's libretto for the opera for Milan.

It arrived, having passed through the Viennese Court censorship, when

The 'grand old man', Johann Adolph Hasse, submitted magnanimously and understandingly to the growing fame of his young rival

the two Mozarts were once more in Italy. They had set out in the middle of August 1771 and, after a short pause at Verona, had travelled directly to Milan. *Ascanio in Alba,* the new opera, a *serenata teatrale,* was to provide a brilliant climax to the festivities for the marriage of Archduke Ferdinand to Princess Maria Riccarda Beatricé of Modena; the other opera performed was *Ruggiero* by Metastasio and Hasse. The Mozarts were full of optimism. Perhaps these Court festivities in Milan would achieve what had been impossible in Vienna. Leopold in particular hoped for this; his son's fame in Italy had made him even more sensitive to circumstances in Salzburg. But here in Milan the whole affair and its chief character, the Archduke, in whose honour Wolfgang's music was written, were all under the Imperial aegis, so that anything was possible and no plans or aspirations were too far-fetched to be considered.

The atmosphere seemed favourable. Good friends, like Manzuoli and Mysliweczek flocked round Mozart as he worked busily on his composition. And the great Hasse himself declared his favourable opinion without envy, ill-will or reservations: 'This boy will send us all into oblivion.' The gaiety and pleasant atmosphere in which the preparations were going forward encouraged Mozart at his work, although it was sometimes difficult to concentrate: 'Above us is a violinist,' he wrote in pretended despair about their lodgings, 'below us is another, on one side is a singing-master who gives lessons in his room, and on the other side an oboist. It is a fine

Count Hieronymus Colloredo

Count Zeill

place to write music in — gives you lots of ideas.' Nevertheless his work, done under such trying conditions, brought him a resounding triumph.

His opera was staged on 17th October. Leopold Mozart wrote in a letter that 'Wolfgang's Serenata has defeated Hasse's opera beyond description.' The fact that the Empress gave him a present and appeared to look on him with favour strengthened his hopes of being offered a post at the Archducal Court while he was still at the Milan festivities. And so the Mozarts remained in Milan until December. But in vain. In fact the young prince had intended to ask the Mozarts, but a letter from the Empress reversed this decision. Her words were anything but flattering. She emphatically warned her son against 'useless people' and gave it as her considered opinion that these people 'drifting round the world like beggars' lowered the status of their occupation.

Though the Mozarts knew nothing of these hard words this failure was nevertheless the first of the dark shadows which fell threateningly over the career which had begun with such promise, such triumphs. True, their hopes were not finally destroyed until a year later when Mozart waited in vain for some message from the Archduke after the successful production on 26th December 1772 of his third and last Milan opera, *Lucio Silla.* The Empress's advice had done its work only too well. It is tragic to think that the sad final result of the three Italian tours was in inverse proportion to their rewarding artistic successes. Had Leopold Mozart misjudged his plan of campaign?

For the time being he had no choice but

Barbara von Mölk's portrait
in the form of a silhouette by an
unknown hand. It is fairly certain that
the sixteen-year-old Mozart
was in love with Barbara,
the daughter of an official at the
Salzburg court

'Air-gun shooting',
one of the Mozart
family's chief pleasures

In Vienna
the Mozarts lodged
in the Tiefer Graben

Empress of Austria,
Marie Theresa

to remain in Salzburg and put away all his dreams.

In Salzburg since their return from the second Italian journey there had been many changes. The old Prince Bishop had died on 16th December 1771. Despite much difficulty and opposition, and contrary to all expectation, Count Hieronymus Colloredo had been appointed to the bishopric on 14th March 1772 and commenced his office on 29th April. He was an energetic man, predisposed towards the ideas of the Age of Enlightenment; on his desk stood busts of Voltaire and Frederick II of Prussia.

In his honour Mozart composed *Il Sogno di Scipione* ('The Dream of Scipio'), an *azione teatrale* to a text by Metastasio; it was performed in Salzburg in May.

This was the beginning of a new period for Mozart in every way. Used to the easy-going old prince, the Mozarts now had to accustom themselves to the severity and punctiliousness of a new overlord. It would be convenient to ascribe to the absolutism of the overlord all the blame for the complications which were soon to arise and which eventually led to a complete breach. But in reality the situation was due to inevitable conflicts between two different generations and outlooks.

Mozart, now sixteen, became a salaried conductor, fulfilled his duties, composed (mainly instrumental works) and enjoyed the not uncritical favour of Count Zeill, the bishop of Chiemsee, who tried to relax the tensions sur-

rounding the young musician. His daily life was diversified by domestic pleasures (principally the traditional air-gun shooting), the old circle of friends and his youthful passions, one of which is believed to have been for Barbara von Mölk. At the first opportunity (when the Prince Bishop went to Vienna) the Mozarts, father and son, hastened to put Salzburg behind them. In reality their journey to Vienna was a mere shot in the dark. They could hardly expect to gain much; perhaps they speculated vaguely on the possibility of obtaining the post of Kapellmeister. But the gracious audience granted them by the Empress was an empty gesture. There remained only several fairly important concerts and visits to old friends and acquaintances, in particular Mesmer, Jean George Noverre, the famous choreographer, and Auenbrugger — artistic and professional families. The Court remained closed to them.

It is significant that in Vienna Mozart worked on compositions which had not been commissioned by anyone, besides the work he had 'brought with him' from Salzburg. He began the music for Philipp Gebler's play *König Thamos* and wrote several string quartets, as he had done some years

The Prannerstrasse, Munich, with the Redoutensaal on the right

A phrase from the Violin Concerto in D major in Mozart's writing (1775)

ago in Italy, without having any particular performance in mind, a very unusual thing for those times. Again, like the Italian journeys, this stay in Vienna in the summer and autumn of 1773 was valuable for its artistic output. The new Viennese style of instrumental writing, epitomised by Joseph Haydn, caught Mozart's interest and stimulated his creative powers.

These new ideas found living expression in the symphonies, serenades and church music which Mozart wrote in the following period in Salzburg. But

Mozart tendered his
resignation in ornate phraseology.
Colloredo accepted it
with sarcastic terseness

the sphere in which he most wanted to conquer, opera, remained impregnable. Then an opportunity came quite unexpectedly from Munich. The Elector of Bavaria, Maximilian III, commissioned him to write an opera for the carnival of 1775; this was *La Finta Giardiniera*, an opera buffa which Mozart altered and presented as *Das Verstellte Gärtnermädchen* in 1780. The libretto by Raniero di Calzabigi, although not a masterpiece by any means, is an eighteenth-century relation of the 'tear-jerkers' of today.

By December 1774 the father and son were in Munich, where they stayed with Canon von Pernat in the cathedral close. Received with the greatest kindness on all sides, Mozart made his début as a church composer with a

Ihro Hochfürstl: Gnaden

Hochwürdigster des Heil: Röm: Reichs
Fürst,

Gnädigster Landes Fürst
und
Herr Herr!

The Elector of Bavaria, Maximilian Joseph III, felt himself bound to give his famous answer: 'There is no vacancy here,' when Mozart applied for a post; Count Seeau too (right) was unable to help him

Misericordias Domini in the unspoken hope of recommending himself to the Bavarian court for future commissions of this kind. He also wrote piano sonatas for von Durnitz, an amateur musician, and entered into a piano-playing contest with the conductor Captain von Beecke at an inn kept by one Herr Albert. But the most important achievement was the opera, which was performed in the Redoutensaal to cries of 'Viva il maestro!'; in the audience sat Nannerl, several Salzburg friends and the poet Schubart. The latter, full of enthusiasm, wrote: 'If Mozart has not been

The 'little cousin'
from Augsburg

forced like a hothouse plant, he must surely become one of the greatest musical composers in the world.'

They enjoyed the festival at Munich to the full before returning to the Salzburg 'slavery'. Mozart plunged into work with passionate enthusiasm, producing divertimenti, serenades, including the serenade for the wedding of the mayor's daughter Elise Haffner, violin concertos, and a piano concerto, much of all this being for the Lodrons and the Lützows, two Salzburg families who were particularly fond of him.

Everything seems to indicate that Mozart was, externally at least, contented. Pupils from the nobility and firm friendships with members of the aristocracy, gentry and intellectual élite — the Schiedenhofens, Barisanis, Gilowskys, Andretters — gave his life at Salzburg the appearance of prosperity. But in his mind he was turning over thoughts and plans for making new contacts through journeys outside Salzburg. Italy was considered and applications made to Padre Martini.

Behind all these deliberations one can sense a certain curious hesitation. *Prelude to* Mozart, who had long since ceased to be a child, cherished different ideas *tragedy* from his father, whose ideals and concepts belonged to a dying age. His son, on the other hand, was maturing various apparently fantastic projects which were symbolic of the outlook of the new generation. He had no intention of waiting long; in particular his relationship to the overlord, which had become irreconcilable, was approaching a crisis. In 1777, after he had been refused permission to take a holiday, Wolfgang Amadeus, with many flourishes, tendered his resignation. It was accepted. On 23rd September 1777 Mozart and his mother took leave of Leopold and Nannerl.

The departure was sad, ominous. They decided to go first to Munich.

Posterity has often blamed the Bavarian Elector for not having a place available for Mozart. And yet his famous answer: 'There is no vacancy here!' was not merely an excuse. But his advice that Mozart should develop his merits in Italy is less understandable. It is easy to see why this 'Italian paroxysm' annoyed Mozart.

His dearest wish was to be able to stay in Munich. Count Seeau, the Elector's Court Chancellor, encouraged this idea. The innkeeper and philanthropist Franz Albert, whose inn 'The Black Eagle' had become a meeting-

Mozart in 1777
— with the Order
of the Golden Spur

The publican Albert
attempted to
persuade Mozart
to stay in Munich

place for the finest characters of the age
and the centre of the city's cultural life,
put forward the interesting suggestion that
Mozart should be guaranteed his basic living
costs by a circle of citizens. Only his
father's letter, expressing doubt as to the
reliability of this, to him, new-fangled way
of supporting oneself, caused Mozart
regretfully to reject this offer. Leopold
Mozart was still dreaming of Court successes — of Mannheim, or even, recently,
of Paris.

So Mozart and his mother, who in these
strange, awesome surroundings played the part of a silent Griselda rather
than a giver of counsel, decided to travel on further. Their visit to the
bourgeois town of Augsburg shook his hopes of being able to find a basis
for his artistic life in the middle classes. However much he recognised and
even welcomed the new era, at that moment he longed to be at a Court.
It was the mockery of the young von Langenmantel, who deliberately pro-
voked the Cavaliere Mozart with his Order, which awoke this longing in
the breast of the hesitant musician.

However there was pleasant news to send to Leopold from his birth-place,
less about Wolfgang's somewhat mixed concert successes than about various
musicians and friends, Johann Andreas Stein, the piano-maker, and many
of his father's old acquaintances. Above all Mozart came to know his relations better — Franz Anton Mozart, the bookbinder, his father's brother,
and his charming, gay daughter, Maria Anna Thekla, his 'little cousin'. 'It
is true that we two suit each other very well, for she is also a bit naughty;
we fool people together, so that we have fun.' Leopold Mozart did not altogether approve of this flirtation. But his cousin, to whom Mozart wrote
several joking letters, was an amusing companion.

Aloysia, one of the 'Weber girls',
was Mozart's great, perhaps
his only, love

Aloisia Lange

It was not too distressing to part from the 'Gothamites', as Leopold Mozart christened his relations, in imitation of Wieland.

At home in Salzburg, Leopold's anxiety about his wife and son was very real. From the now silent lodgings he deluged them with well-intentioned advice and long letters, instructions and cautions against his son's sometimes over-hasty decisions and actions. He was not with them, could not direct them, help them or tell them what to do, and consequently he feared the worst — all the more so when he heard rumours of his son's having behaved foolishly in Hohenaltheim, the country seat of Prince Kraft Ernst of Öttingen and Wallerstein. Reproaches and impressive admonitions flowed from his pen — not for the last time.

The next stop was Mannheim. The francophile Court of Elector Carl Theodor, a cultured if unprincipled man, exercised a strong attraction. It was the ruler's aim to make Mannheim a centre of learning and culture. The famed Mannheim orchestra, for instance, in which eminent soloists played under the baton of Christian Cannabich, embodied the principles of the new style of instrumental playing. Abt Vogler, a man of many skills, was also at the Court. The opera flourished. Gottsched's works on German style and language were

The Serrarius
house, where
Mozart lived
while in
Mannheim

being discussed, and perpetuated in the Deutsche Gesellschaft. By fostering
modern writing Mannheim was to become the cultural centre of south-west
Germany. And the town's fame was justified still further by the presence and
work of men of the calibre of Gemmingen, the 'father of Germany' and Dalberg; it was confirmed once and for all by the production of *The Robbers*
which the young Schiller wrote for it.

Mozart wanted to become part of this inspiring activity. There were various reasons why he never achieved it. Everything should not be attributed to the beginning of the official opposition, for which Vogler was partly responsible. Mozart was himself not without prejudices and lost many an opportunity through his own foolish tongue, although he had plenty of friends and supporters.

Christoph Martin Wieland

But something had entered his life which made these winter months in Mannheim a source of inward unrest and strengthened his desire to stay in the city. But this desire, too, aroused his father's opposition, so that he felt torn between duty and inclination. Leopold was pre-occupied by monetary worries and was caused much heart-searching by his son's changeability. For he suspected what was going on in Mannheim.

Mozart had fallen violently in love. Aloysia Weber, a young and gifted singer, had bewitched him. She was the daughter of Fridolin Weber, who had settled down as prompter in the theatre after a lifetime of remarkable wanderings; his brother was the father of Carl Maria von Weber. There were three daughters in all at Mannheim of whom one, Constanze, was to play an important part in Mozart's future life; another daughter and a son are shrouded in impenetrable obscurity. If one can believe her lover's account, Aloysia's future was impeded by the straitened circumstances of the family, which was openly governed by the mother, Cäcilia Weber.

Mozart kept his feelings a secret from his own mother. But his father read between the lines of his son's letter with penetrating accuracy and was immediately aware of the situation. Without a moment's hesitation he told his son what he thought, complained and ordered him to give up such ideas. Mozart, who was giving concerts with Aloysia, answered with rash plans, pipe-dreams about new Italian tours, weddings and gorgeous castles in the air. It was a hard task to rid his son's mind of the Weber girl. For this love, which transformed the innermost elements of Mozart's life, was deep and true.

Mozart, certainly not averse to feminine charms, has often been accused of being a philanderer. Tales were told of 'affairs below stairs' — and not only as anecdotes or romanticised stories; such rumours were being circulated immediately after his death and Beethoven was one of those who believed them. But in fact there is no more harm in the letters to his cousin, whose frivolous tone can easily be misinterpreted, than in Mozart's personal remarks to the 'Jungfrau Mizerl' when he reminds her of her negligee or, immediately after Mannheim, assures Rosalie Joly, or 'Sallerl', of his love and fidelity. The 'adored

Abbé Vogler

ones' — one well over sixty and the other some ten years younger — understood the joke perfectly well. And when he flirted with Rosa Cannabich of Mannheim or turned Gustl Wendling's head with flattery, it was all merely the exuberance of a highly impressionable, highly gifted young man.

But, however difficult his position, he never lost his sense of humour — or his lust for work. During the Mannheim period he composed a few piano sonatas in the local style and some other pieces.

Mannheim offered plenty of excitement, although it was not easy for Mozart to steer a clear course between the various parties in the intrigues which beset the atmosphere of the Court. He was deeply impressed by the German opera *Günther von Schwarzburg* by Ignaz Holzbauer; this was generally hailed as the dawn of a new theatrical era and aroused Schiller's enthusiasm. On the other hand, he was not attracted by Holzbauer's rival, the conceited Abt Vogler — another reason why his prospects could not be very hopeful. He got on best with his friends from the orchestra, Johann Baptist Wendling, August Ramm and Cannabich. And then there were his 'scholars', the 'Indian' Dejean and the daughter of the Court Counsellor, Serrarius, in whose house he and his rather solitary mother found friendly lodgings.

From the literary point of view Mannheim was the scene of an interesting meeting. Mozart met no less a person than Christoph Martin Wieland, the great poet and man of letters who was staying in the town with the composer Anton Schweitzer to work on the opera, *Rosemunde*. Mozart looked forward with some apprehension to his meeting with this man who was held in such high esteem by the whole of the Mozart family. His description of the event is delightful. Unlike the ecstatic Mannheim folk who hardly dared open their mouths in the presence of the great poet and accepted each of his statements as an oracle, Mozart was at first disappointed. He took exception to Wieland's coarse behaviour and was amused at his thick speech and 'continuous glassy stare'. But he could not deny that he had, 'as we all know, an amazing brain'. The constraint between the two men was dissipated when Wieland listened to Mozart's playing. 'It is real good fortune for me,' remarked the poet, 'to have met you here.'

Mannheim was probably the most important single episode in Mozart's early development. His opposition to his father's authority, even when it was exercised from afar, became a battle for his right to his own opinions and autonomy. His whole character and emotions were confused and disturbed. He hovered between decision and indecision and finally acceded to his father's

Mozart's mother died in Paris in the Rue du Gros Chenet
(centre of plan) in 1778; her funeral took place
in the church of St Eustache *(top right)*

Paris ce 3 juillet 1778

inexorable will: 'Away with you to Paris, and as speedily as may be; put yourself in the company of the great — aut Caesar aut nihil!' It was the beginning of the tragic rupture of the friendship between father and son.

Mozart certainly did not have all the right on his side but in this instance he was wiser, or at least less gullible, than his father. Leopold still believed that the triumph of his child prodigy would repeat itself in Paris, the centre of the cultural world at that time. Wolfgang, however, knew better. It was clear to him that he himself had grown up and that the world around him had changed.

With a heavy heart he left Mannheim — and Aloysia — with his mother on 14th March 1778.

But Paris was now in a ferment. The first cracks were appearing in the structure of the *ancien régime*. Political and social life were disrupted by the struggle between the dying rationalism and the new movement towards equality and romanticism whose outstanding figure was Rousseau. The quarrel between the supporters of Gluck and Piccini had developed into a conflict of philosophies.

Mozart, who had been directed to Grimm by his father, was not inclined to become involved in these differences of opinion. Grimm, ever a convinced supporter of the Italian school, felt himself personally insulted by his protégé's

On 3rd July 1778 Mozart sent
the Abbé Bullinger this letter
informing him of his mother's death

Thus Anna Maria Mozart, their quiet,
cheerful mother, lived on in the minds of the
family. (After a posthumous portrait)

lack of interest and let him drop. Mozart's frankness seemed to him just as
incomprehensible as his stubbornness. Once again the mutual antipathy, disguised as frosty politeness, was merely an unreconcilable difference between
two generations.

Mozart's loneliness was made bearable by the presence in Paris of his Mannheim friends, including Wendling and Ramm. It was they who helped a little
to introduce Mozart to the musical life of Paris. He came into contact with
François Joseph Gossec and received some work for the 'Concerts Spirituels'

The funeral for Mozart's mother
was held in the
Church of St Eustache

79

from Jean le Gros. Noverre, who was again living in Paris, wrote the choreography for the ballet *Les Petits Riens,* which was performed to Mozart's music on 11th June 1778. There was talk of plans for a French opera. The Duke of Guines, an amateur flautist to whose daughter Mozart was giving composition lessons, made an offer for his services. Perhaps something might have come of the overtures of this favourite of Marie Antoinette, to whom Mozart had proposed marriage at five years of age. Perhaps . . .

Everything was undecided. Mozart seemed to be paralysed, immovable and incapable of taking any initiative. His gloomy lodging in the rue du Gros Chenet were not calculated to re-awaken his gaiety and cheerfulness. His mother, occupying her long hours of solitude with needlework, remained silent. She became ill and recovered only slowly: in June she was still unable to get up.

His mother's death On 3rd July 1778, one day after Rousseau's death, Mozart received the hardest blow of his life up to that point: his mother died.

On 4th July the funeral service was held in the Church of St Eustache and the body buried in one of its three cemeteries — probably the Cimetière Saint-

The famous Sonata in A major is one of the
few works written while Mozart was in Paris

Madame
d'Epinay

One of Mozart's
dedications (1778)

Jean-Porte-Latine and not the Cimetière des Innocents as has been thought in
the past. Mozart and the horn-player, Heina, who had given much assistance
during the illness, were the only two mourners.

At this moment, when despair broke pitilessly over him and his solitude was
painfully brought home to him, Mozart reached his true maturity and greatness.

For the first time, completely alone in a strange city, which to him seemed
cold and even hostile, he was obliged to take all the responsibility for himself.
It is moving to read his letters to his father, in which he tries to prepare him
for the dreadful news by a kind lie, and to the Abbé Bullinger, an old Salzburg
friend to whom he revealed the truth. Even more moving is the suspicion
which had gripped Leopold and which in the end caused him to accuse his son
of being to blame for his mother's death.

For Mozart this must have been an almost unbearable period. Something of
what he must have suffered can be heard in the violin and piano sonatas which
he finished in Paris. It must have been a great comfort to meet his old friend
Johann Christian Bach again. With him in St Germain, in the palace of
Maréchal Louis de Noailles he could forget his misery and the hostility of the

The fountain of
Salzburg Cathedral

Aloysia Lange was a successful
prima donna when she rejected
Mozart's advances

strange metropolis in music and conversation.

He had found refuge in the house belonging to Grimm and his mistress, Louise d'Epinay, in the rue de la Chaussée d'Antin. Grimm expressed himself willing to help. But in the end their irreconcilable differences of opinion were leading to an open quarrel. Only the efforts of the good-natured Madame d'Epinay prevented a serious conflict. After all the discussions, in which in the end Leopold Mozart took a part, Mozart set off for the sad journey back to Salzburg on 16th September 1778. Since nothing else was possible, he was ready to return to his post in the cathedral city.

The journey was long and roundabout: they stopped at Nancy, Strasbourg and, for a longish period, at Mannheim. In the few months he had been away there had been several changes. Carl Theodor, who had acceded to the electorate of Bavaria, had moved to Munich with the greater part of his Court — including Mozart's musician friends and Aloysia. Nevertheless, Mozart stayed for some time in Mannheim, drawn by a theatrical problem — the composition for the melodrama *Semiramis* by Gemmingen, a new dramatic genre which was being discussed in the newly founded Mannheim theatre directed by Dalberg. Was there perhaps some opportunity for him in Mannheim? Leopold Mozart once

The shrine in Maria Plain

Emanuel Schikaneder, the great man
of the theatre, has been maligned by
his posthumous reputation

again laid down an emphatic embargo:
'I hope that this letter will not catch you
in Mannheim and that, since you will
have received my answer of the 19th, if
you are still in Mannheim you will leave
by the first mail, and that is the reason why
I am sending you this second letter. I am
tired of your projects with which you
have destroyed the excellent plans I have
often had; which you can never realise
because you can't — or won't — think
over anything in cold blood and without
prejudice; often it is true that you can't
because you are carried away in an in-
stant by the fire of your youth and the
flattering suggestions made to you by
this or that person, and see everything as
gold which is in fact only tinsel. In particular, your taking up the post here . . .
is the only certain way of getting to
Italy again . . .'

So, on Christmas Day, Mozart set off with the prelate of Kaisheim, with whom
he had been staying for a short time, for Munich. But Aloysia, now in a better
professional position, needed him no longer and turned her back on him. This
was the greatest sorrow of the whole sorrowful journey. He could not count
on a post in Munich, despite a gracious audience granted him by the Elector's
wife. In the middle of January 1779, Mozart returned to Salzburg, disappointed, unsuccessful, rich only in experience and debts. Leopold was understanding enough to make no reproaches whatsoever. The prodigal son was
received with all possible love and affection, not only at home but also by the
Prince Bishop who gave him back his position as Court Organist in the cathedral. Mozart, as Court and church musician, composed litanies, masses — including the Coronation Mass, presumably for the coronation of the image of
the Virgin in Maria Plain — and church voluntaries, and was able to show that
at least his roaming round the world had not been in vain. His mental and
artistic transformation, of a piece with his growing up as a person, revealed

itself particularly in his new symphonic works, serenades, divertimenti and concerti. The most important part of the Salzburg work done between 1778 and 1780 was, however, in a different sphere. Even if it did not reach beyond the planning stage or first beginnings, it can nevertheless be seen from his manipulation of the material that Mozart's heart was not really in his work for the Court. His mind was taken up by something for which the Salzburg Court offered no opportunity — the theatre.

He began to write an 'operetta' which was later called *Zaïde.* Schachtner had adapted the text from an old *singspiel, Das Serail.* The theatre company managed by Johann Heinrich Böhm, later to become one of Mozart's most enthusiastic supporters, was to perform it during their visit to Salzburg in 1779. At least the work stimulated the troupe of Bohemian players. Mozart, who at this time was also reconsidering Gebler's play *König Thamos,* grasped gratefully every chance of being near the theatre.

Since the Mozarts' house near the Hannibalgarten was near to the theatre, Mozart had many opportunities of coming into contact with the visiting company. Evening after evening he sat in the theatre and conversed with the principals, partly from a desire to interrupt the humdrum round of Salzburg daily life and breathe the invigorating air of the outside world. For in his own home there were always the same people round him — his 'little cousin' had long since gone home — and conversation always consisted of an exchange of the same thoughts and opinions.

In the autumn of 1780 Emanuel Schikaneder came to Salzburg with his troupe of players. Schikaneder, who has been unjustly and excessively slandered in the past, was simultaneously actor, producer and playwright; he was welcomed at the Mozarts' house and even entered so far

One of Mozart's frivolous letters to the 'little cousin'

The Sonneck house *(fourth from left)*, where Mozart completed
Idomeneo, stood before the gates of the old castle at Munich

into intimacy with the family that he was invited to join in the traditional
air-gun shooting. He had brought a varied and up-to-date repertoire with
him: besides the 'stock' authors of the day — Leisewitz, Gotter, Iffland, Gemmingen, Clodius — there were Shakespeare's *Hamlet*, which made a profound
impression on Mozart, Lessing's *Emilia Galotti* and Beaumarchais' *Barbier de
Seville*, with which the Mozarts were already familiar. For another company
had already played Shakespeare and Lessing and even Goethe *(Clavigo)* in
Salzburg. When Mozart went to Munich in November he asked his sister to
send him a list of all the comedies which were played in his absence.

His first contact with Schikaneder led to a modest degree of collaboration
between the two; Mozart was briefed to write an additional aria for Gozzi's
Die Schlaflosen Nächte.

Mozart, surrounded by so much theatre, had no need to content himself with being a spectator. Once again it was Munich which offered him a holiday and a brief period of liberty. Whether it pleased him or not, the resentful Prince Bishop could not refuse the invitation from the Elector Carl Theodor of Bavaria for Mozart to write an opera for the Munich carnival of 1781. One of his subordinates, the Salzburg Court Chaplain Abbate Giambattista Varesco, undertook to convert the old play of *Idomeneo* by Danchet and Campra into a libretto. Thus, as he was on the spot, Mozart could work in direct collaboration with his librettist, even though he was not always in entire agreement with Varesco's dramatic ideas.

With the prospect before him of his dearest wish being fulfilled, Mozart's work almost did itself. The enthusiasm with which, in his critical examination of the structure of the new drama, he calculated the exact value of his own ideas shows that he was now an independent artist in his own right and very well aware of the importance of the moment. In October 1780 everything was ready. Mozart undertook the awkward journey to Munich in order to direct things on the spot. *Idomeneo* was finished in his lodgings there while the first rehearsals were already in progress.

There were no difficulties or intrigues to be expected and everything took its normal course peacefully and reassuringly. From his lofty position the

Left: Dorothea Wendling, the Ilia in the first performance of *Idomeneo*
Above: Elisabeth Wendling, the Elektra in the first performance of *Idomeneo*

IDOMENEO.
DRAMMA
PER
MUSICA
DA RAPPRESENTARSI
NEL TEATRO NUOVO DI
CORTE
PER COMANDO
DI S. A. S E.

CARLO TEODORO
Come Palatino del Rheno, Duca dell'
alta, e bafsa Baviera, e del Palatinato
Superiore, etc. etc. Archidapifero,
et Elettore, etc. etc.

NEL CARNOVALE

1 7 8 1.

La Poesia è del Signor Abate Gianbattista Varesco
Capellano di Corte di S. A. R. l'Arcivescovo, e Principe di Salisburgo.
La Musica è del Signor Maestro Wolfgango Amadeo Mozart Academico di Bologna, e di Verona, in
fin attual servizio di S. A. R. l'Arcivescovo, e Principe
di Salisburgo.
La Traduzione è del Signor Andrea Schachtner,
pure in attual servizio di S. A. R. l'Arcivescovo, e
Principe di Salisburgo.

MONACO.
Aprefso Francesco Giuseppe Thuille.

The first performance of
Idomeneo took place in
Cuvilliés' Residenztheater

A printed edition of the libretto
of *Idomeneo* was published
in the year of its first performance

Elector smiled down benignly. Count Seeau,
now one of the new members of the Court
commissariat, was kind and helpful. The nobility and gentry showed its most encouraging
side. Cannabich did his best, the orchestra and
singers were nothing if not obliging and un-
temperamental. Mozart wrote one or two letters home about Varesco's poetasting which
was not entirely to his liking and which he
altered to suit his own better dramatic in-
stincts. But the only thing which caused him
real concern was the performance of two of
the main rôles — in particular the Idomeneo of
Anton Raaft who was no longer a young man. Mozart was obliged to give him
instructions as to his breathing. The other worry was the Idamante of Vin-
cenzo del Prato, who was unfortunately lacking in musical feeling. On the
other hand the two female rôles gave Mozart immense pleasure: they were
sung by the Wendling sisters, Dorothea and Liesl.

Mozart refused to allow himself to be distracted by anyone and devoted
himself entirely to his opera, working on both the musical and production
sides. Every rehearsal impressed on him, on the performers and on the Elector,
who was sometimes in the audience, the consciousness that they were dealing
with something quite out of the ordinary. To his father's anxiety that he

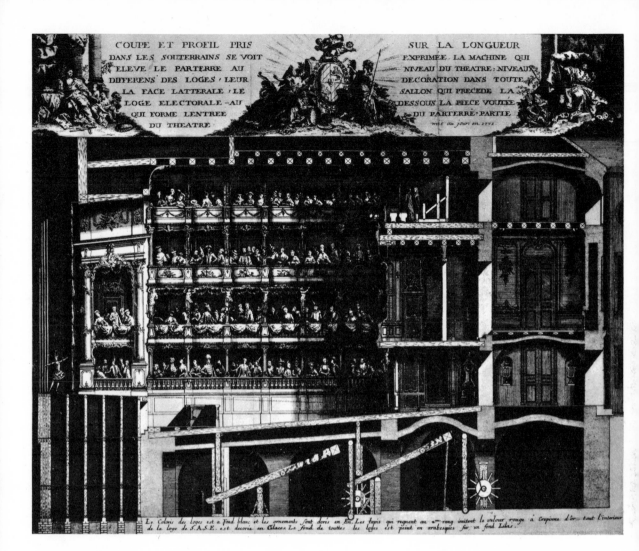

would forget the 'unmusical public' and the 'popular style for the curiosity-mongers' in his composition he answered with the laconic statement: 'In my opera there is music for every kind of man — always excepting the curiosity-mongers.'

Time was pressing and the third act was still unwritten. 'My head and hands are so full of the third act that it would be no surprise if I were to turn into a third act myself. It is costing me more trouble than a whole opera, for there is hardly a scene in it which is not of extraordinary interest.'

This was at the beginning of January 1781. The ballet music which was needed in addition had yet to be written, so that everybody was pleased when

the first performance was postponed. On 26th January his father and sister arrived to witness the dress rehearsal.

On 29th January the first performance finally took place in the Residency Theatre, the beautiful building designed by Cuvilliés. In the public announcement only the stage designer Lorenz Quaglio was named: otherwise it said merely that the 'words, music and translation [by Schachtner] originated from Salzburg'.

One gets the impression that all who took part in it were aware of the significance of the occasion. For the whole conception of the work, an *opera seria*, must have shown that it represented a step into new operatic territory. The old form of the baroque drama and the new ideas of the early nineteenth-century generation were combined in an exuberant superabundance of musical and dramatic expressions, stimulated more by Shakespeare than by Gluck.

Mozart's entire ambition in Vienna was concentrated on playing before the Emperor Joseph II

Josef and Aloysia Lange. When Mozart went to Vienna his erstwhile love had already settled there after marrying the Court actor, Lange

In 1781 Mozart lived for a time in the same house as his overlord

Mozart had found his voice. The way was open for any future developments. But he still did not look forward with any pleasure to the future. 'Upon my honour, the prince and the nobility, not Salzburg itself, become ever more unbearable.' It made him melancholy merely to think of Salzburg. Perhaps — how many times he had already said 'Perhaps'! — the time had come when Munich, the town of which he was so fond, had a vacancy to offer. Now he was a proven master, no longer a young applicant who might possibly be of service. As he had done before, he again took his leave with church music, this time the Munich Kyrie which, like the Horn Serenades, shows a new Mozart. He presented the latter to the soloists of the orchestra; similarly various arias, songs and the oboe quartet were donated to friends in Munich.

But did he have to go back to Salzburg? The six-week holiday had long since

The Kärntnertor
Theatre

been exceeded. Mozart was lucky. The Prince Bishop had left for Vienna with the Court — Maria Theresa had died in November — to pay their respects to the emperor. So he could stay in Munich and enjoy the rest of the carnival, besides keeping an eye open for possibilities, a position of which even his father approved.

But then, like a bolt from the blue, came a message from the Prince Bishop ordering his Court Organist to come to Vienna immediately.

On 16th March 1781 he arrived in 'pianoland', a Salzburg Court servant at his master's beck and call. True, he had the honour of lodging in the German House, where the prince also was staying. But his freedom was severely restricted. After much deliberation, he decided that he should attempt an audience with the emperor: 'I would so much like to run through my opera for him and then play fugues.' With great difficulty he had managed to arrange a public concert. The Viennese public, not easily pleased, had applauded vigorously.

And then he had old friends in Vienna, including the Webers. The father was now dead. Aloysia, now married to Lange, a Court actor, was no longer a danger. In his mind Mozart already felt at home in Vienna, the Vienna which he saw as the best place in the world for his work.

Then came the Prince Bishop's order to return home. Mozart refused to obey. The long-pent-up self-suppression finally exploded. His request to resign remained unanswered. Count Arco stepped in. He submitted his resignation a second and a third time. Finally it came to an angry scene on 8th June 1781. One word led to another. The composer was dismissed with a kick by the Prince Bishop. Trembling, almost ill with anger, Mozart swore revenge; his dignity and honour had been severely wounded: 'A man is noble by virtue of his character and, if I am not a Count, I have probably more honour within me than many a man who is; and whether anybody is a lackey or a Count, if he insults me he is a cur.' Leopold Mozart was thunderstruck by the news,

Catarina Cavalieri

Valent: Adamberger

The two principals in the first performance of *Il Seraglio*

Osmin's aria
in Mozart's
handwriting

von Apperst in O.Ö. notarie majorennis, wofnt
laut Attestat 3 Jahr zu Mötzlein d dorst N° 34.

Tertio Dño Philipp Nergunr, new
Schumacher auf der Wieden N° 51, et
Dño Peter Neumacher Bürgyrn zu
Mötzlein dorst N° 2.

der woflEndle H Wolfgang Adam
Mozart, ein Kapellmeister, ledig,
geb. von Salzburg, des H Leopold Mozart,
Kapellmeisters allda, et Maria Anna
ux. ej. nata Bertl nße Söhn, cons. ab
exc. Regim. tulit, wofnt durmalen 12 Tag
nß den hohen Brucke N° 387, vor sein 5
Monat in gerben, und vor dorjenen
1 Jahr unter den Aufklaubnen beim Aug
Gottes, übrigens 16 Monat statt allsier,
ita testatus dñus tutor, et testis Dña

Mit der woflEdlen H. Konstanzia
Weberin, geb. von Zell in U.Ö., des H
Fridlin Weber, K.K. HofMusici und
et Cäcilia ux. nata Stamin nße Dochter,
cons. tutor. a judicio Mareschal aulico tulit,
wofnt 2 Jahr im Joter beim Aug Gottes
N° 577, ita testatur tutor, et testis.

Tertis Dño Titl H Johann Thorwart,
K.K. Hofdienkhout Revisor, et H H
Johann Cetto v. Eronstorf, K.K. n.ö. Regie-
rungsrath, et Dño H Franz Gilowsky,
Medicinä Doctor.

der nße. Gottfried Grüppel, ein
Naumeisterbürger, geb. von Wittard-
bach in Böhmen, des Gottfried Grüppel, geb.
et Maria Elisabetha ux. nata Wagnern nße Söhn,

Mozart's marriage certificate. He married Constanzia Weber before receiving notice of his father's consent

Ticket of admittance for a 'Dilettante Concert' which Mozart gave in the Augarten, Vienna

tried to set things right, reproved his son and reproached him for the rumours which reached his ears as to his altered situation. Mozart remained firm. His enforced departure from Salzburg marked the final break with the past.

Now that he stood on his own feet, it behoved him to move quickly. Where could he find a niche for himself? Where else but in the theatre? Once again he set himself to study the stage with enormous enthusiasm and thirst for knowledge. The new national opera house, only opened in 1778, was bound to draw his attention. Here, where the concept of a national theatre was transformed into reality, if only for a short period, the new artistic genre of the *singspiel,* or opera with some spoken dialogue, developed, although the first works produced there could not furnish a really convincing proof of its potentialities.

On 9th June 1781, Mozart was in a position to give his father at least some good news, amongst much that was less pleasant: something was afoot. Count Rosenberg had commissioned him to look out some suitable material for an opera which the emperor was eager that he should write. In the end, Bretzner's comedy *Belmont und Constanze* was chosen. Gottlieb Stephanie arranged a libretto from this play for *Die Entführung aus dem Serail (Il Seraglio).* Mozart was delighted by this 'Turkish subject'. But it was the human side of the piece, about which Mozart gave much valuable information as to his aesthetic and dramatic views in his letters, which raised the *singspiel* as a new theatrical genre to the level of the 'straight' theatre of the day, as written by Lessing, Goethe and Schiller.

The first performance of the *Seraglio* on 16th July 1782 was not achieved entirely without opposition. Catarina Cavalieri sang Constanze, Valentin Adamburger taking the part of Belmonte. Further performances resulted in a re-

Greiner, Jacquin and, in particular, Gottfried van Swieten were Mozart's friends and patrons in Vienna

sounding success. Even the emperor was pleased although he is said to have remarked: 'Too fine for our ears, and a terrible lot of notes, my dear Mozart!' This observation, whether fictitious or not, shows that Mozart had freed himself from the ideals of Italian opera and had at last found his own ideal which was beginning to amaze his contemporaries.

The production of the opera was followed by yet another drama, this time one of reality and tending more towards tragedy than comedy.

Even before his dismissal from the Salzburg Court, Mozart had been lodging in the Webers' house. Madame Weber, a lady who was fond of drink, and who had already married off one daughter, Aloysia, to Lange, watched in calculating silence while some feeling appeared to grow up between Mozart and her other daughter, Constanze. Leopold Mozart feared the worst and urged his son to give up the acquaintance. In the autumn Mozart did in fact move. But local gossip had already begun and with it the machinations of the Weber girls' guardian, Johannes Thorwart. While the young folk were ablaze with love the old lady suddenly took a hand and forbade Mozart the house — unless he were prepared either to sign a formal promise of marriage or to pay Madame Weber a regular annuity for the rest of her life.

Constanze   From Salzburg Leopold Mozart heard of these affairs with great misgivings.

Von Trattnern

J. H. F. Müller

The nobleman von
Trattnern, a self-made man,
opened his doors
to Mozart.
Leopold Mozart was
friendly with Müller,
a writer and actor

He put up a stubborn fight for his paternal rights, but his son would not give in. Although difficulties also arose with Constanze, he did all he could to dissipate his father's distaste with soft words. Constanze, for her part tired of her mother's oppression, submitted to being 'abducted' to the house of Baroness Waldstätten. Mozart did not want to marry without his father's blessing. Nevertheless he was in fact joined in marriage to 'J. Constanzia Weber, spinster', in St Stephen's on 4th August 1782 before he received Leopold's grudging consent.

To the end of his life Constanze was Mozart's 'dearest, best little wife', despite the rather mixed judgment which has been passed on her by posterity. Whether she was really conscious of whom or what she had married it is impossible to say. But it must be said in her praise that it was she who, with surprising sense, encouraged Mozart to perfect himself in a form which he was attempting at this time — the fugue.

Since Bach was accorded the greatest respect and admiration at the Austrian Imperial Court and Handel's work was promoted in Vienna by Gottfried von Smieten it is not really surprising that Mozart — like Haydn — was attracted by the polyphonic glories of the earlier part of the century. But the amazing thing is that when he had already reached a level of near-perfection as a composer he should have been willing, and indeed eager, to go back to the beginning with a new branch of his art, in all humility.

The success of *Il Seraglio,* echoes of which reached far beyond Vienna itself, strengthened his position in the city, even if he was still not accorded the appreciation due to him. He gave concerts. He played in musical contests with Muzio Clementi, who took him for a valet on account of his elegant clothes. His early intentions of going to Paris or London were shelved in favour of more certain hopes of a post as musical director in Vienna. But he had not reckoned with the deep-seated rivalry he would arouse, nor with the opposition of the great Antonio Salieri, who basked in the emperor's favour. The Court remained closed to him. It seems now, reviewing the course of events from our present standpoint, that it was Mozart's historical mission to create the type of the independent artist. The position which was forced on him between Court commissions and his own free will was symptomatic of the position of the whole of the new generation.

Mozart circulated among the nobility with nonchalance — the Thuns, the Lichnowskys, the Hatzfelds, the Greiners, the Galitzins — not yet demanding respect as of right, like Beethoven, but conscious of his value and dignity. In the company of Jacquin, who became one of his best friends, or of van Swieten, he found understanding and sympathy. But at first the public recognition received by the other great ones of the Viennese musical world was denied him. His chosen circle of patrons and disciples was composed mainly — and the more so the longer he lived in Vienna — of cultured people and musicians. He moved further and further away from aristocratic circles, of whom Hatzfeld was the most sympathetic to him, and towards those of science and art. As a man and artist he found refuge with actors like Johann Heinrich Müller, Stephanie, Lange, his brother-in-law, scholars like the mineralogist Ignaz von Born and various writers of the new age. Thus it was not the 'officials', the

Portrait of Mozart by Josef Lange, showing him as serious, inward-looking. 'He was always good-humoured,' wrote his sister-in-law Sophie, 'but at the best of times very thoughtful'

From Baron Wetzlar's house the young couple 'made an untimely move to a bad lodging in the Kohlmarkt'

St Peter's
in Salzburg

authorities, who recognised him but those people in whom the outlooks and ideas of the new age were fermenting. This explains why in 1783 Mozart tried to make contact with Freemasonry and its humanistic doctrine. It also explains Mozart's artistic career from this point and the fact that he concentrated on opera. His frequently emphasised creed, 'expressive gusto', was more than an aesthetic or stylistic idea. It represents in a large measure his demand for a new evaluation of art — made at the same time and in the same degree as Goethe's similar demand. Lange's description of Mozart at this time, the most lifelike of all the descriptions of him, shows an already ill, introspective, mature man. Nothing suggests the ideally handsome favourite of the gods. His facial expression was serious and even tense. Mozart, though happy in his young marriage, was nevertheless driven by intellectual unrest and human longings. Moreover he was for the most part in financial trouble. Drawn towards a gay, social life and an extravagant mode of living, often above his means, Mozart certainly deserved some of the blame for his own distresses. In 1782 he changed his lodgings no less than four times.

However — and this is a curious thing — it was during this period of restlessness that the turning-point in his artistic career occurred. A change of style was apparent in his instrumental works. It owed something to his new acquaintance with Joseph Haydn's music and his fascinated return to the works of Bach and Handel. His restless mind embarked on yet a new voyage of discovery.

It was Constanze who had urged Mozart on when he found himself drawn towards the contrapuntal music of the baroque age, an attraction which had been aroused by van Swieten's Sunday musical parties. The first immediate result of this new-found affinity with Bach and Handel was a work which was also connected with Constanze in another way — the Mass in C Minor. It sprang from a promise which he was bound to keep: when he had been suing for Constanze's hand he had vowed a Mass, as a thank-offering, if he should succeed in making her his wife.

Thus the first months of the Vienna period were equally critical from both the artistic and personal standpoints. In both Mozart had taken his own decisions, quite independently, and carried them out himself. The whole of the rest of his life illustrates the importance of the steps taken at this time.

Only one question concerning the Mass in C Minor remains unanswered. It remained unfinished, like nearly all the works which were specifically written for Constanze. Should one draw any conclusions from this? Or did they remain unfinished for artistic reasons? From his letters we know that, although he was not a *connoisseur d'hommes* or misanthropical cynic like his father, he was a very shrewd observer. His style of writing varies according to the character and conduct of the recipient. His letters to Constanze, his wife, are permeated with love and longing and the desire for security. The only remaining letter to Aloysia, written in Italian, is classically formal, without any of his usual light touches. His letters to the 'little cousin' are frivolous and suggestive, because she was agreeable to 'that sort of thing'. But in the letters to his wife can be seen all the trust and confidence that bound him to her; this grew out of the

Constanze Mozart

Mozart's sister, Nannerl

knowledge of the common fate which, despite one or two lapses, Constanze shared with him bravely and even light-heartedly until she was his only remaining friend.

For Constanze's sake and to conciliate Leopold Mozart they went for a holiday to Salzburg. A succession of adverse circumstances had delayed their departure for a long period. The last impediment was the birth to Constanze of a son. Once again misunderstandings arose when it came to naming the new-born baby. Mozart had promised his still offended father to call it Leopold after him, but Baron von Wetzlar, Mozart's landlord, expressed a wish to see the child called Raimund. The suggestion of a compromise, that the baby should be given both names, did little to dispel the grandfather's ill-humour. It might have come to a pointless quarrel but before the Mozarts returned from Salzburg the 'fat little baby' had died in Vienna. Its parents returned to find only a grave.

In the end their visit to Leopold in Salzburg in no way fulfilled the hopes which the young couple had set on it. The position improved, but not enough. Leopold Mozart and the good-natured Nannerl, who had given up the possibility of a fine career for her brother's sake, failed to discard their jealous reserve towards Constanze.

Nevertheless time passed merrily, with laughter and amusements of all kinds. The entries in Nannerl's diary, to which her brother added his own jocose

One of Nannerl's rings and her visiting card after she had married into the nobility. The card is written in Nannerl's hand

In 1784 Mozart made up his mind to keep a record of his works

comments, show that all the family were in a good humour. They say nothing, however, of the first performance in St Peter's of the Mass in C Minor, whose date is traditionally held to be 23rd August 1783. Nor do they mention that in this performance Mozart conducted and Constanze sang. The affair is not noted until a later date.

When the young Mozarts left Leopold and Nannerl it was, as it turned out, for the last time. What must have been Mozart's thoughts as he watched Maria Plain and the Salzburg fortress on its hill dwindling away behind him? He had been received in Salzburg without resentment. Indeed Varesco, remembering the success of *Idomeneo*, had pressed a new plan for an opera, *L'oca del Cairo* ('The Goose of Cairo') into his hand. But with his present experience in opera work he could take little interest in the project. No doubt he chuckled as he remembered how he had amused himself by composing for the Prince Bishop various duets under the name of Michael Haydn, from whom they had been ordered; the Prince Bishop had suspected nothing. For that alone the journey was worth while.

At the end of November they were back in Vienna, after having made short stays in Lanbach and Linz, where Mozart wrote the Linz Symphony. 'My wife and I,' wrote Mozart from there to his father, 'kiss your hands and beg your forgiveness for having inconvenienced you for so long.'

The studies he had begun before the journey were now continued. His new style, influenced by Bach and

The house in the Schulergasse where *Figaro* was written

The friendship between
Haydn and Mozart is comparable
only with that between
Goethe and Schiller

Handel, became even more profound and significant through his absorption of the fantastic character of Carl Philipp Emanuel Bach's music. Along with his work his reputation increased. Mozart began to have a position in Vienna. Giuseppe Sarti and Giovanni Paesiello, the rulers of the Italian opera of the city, judged him worthy of their professional recognition. With subscription concerts and composition, 1784 was rich in achievement and success, although a serious illness cast a dark ominous shadow over the gay life that Mozart was attempting to build up in the new order of things. Doctor Barisani, the son of a Salzburg friend, came to his assistance.

But his stalwart lust for life and fierce joy in working were still stronger than his premonition of death, which Mozart always looked forward to fearlessly as a friend and the means to 'happiness'. His old light-heartedness returned when he was called upon to congratulate his sister upon her marriage to the respectably mature Baron of Berchtold zu Sonnenberg: it was a marriage of convenience, to which the good-natured Nannerl agreed after she had been forced to suppress her inclination for Captain d'Ippold. Being now allied to such a noble family and having acquired such respectable pretensions, Mozart thought it necessary to create an equally dignified background for his own life. In his house in the Schulergasse near St Stephen's, where *Figaro* was written and the young Beethoven came for lessons, he was able to arrange musical parties to which more illustrious guests could also be invited.

SEI
QUARTETTI
PER DUE VIOLINI, VIOLA, E VIOLONCELLO.
*Composti e Dedicati
al Signor*
GIUSEPPE HAYDN
*Maestro di Cappella di S.A.
il Principe d'Esterhazy &c &c
Dal Suo Amico*
W.A. MOZART
Opera X.
*In Vienna presso Artaria Comp.
Mercanti ed Editori di Stampe Musica.
e Carte Geografiche.*

One of these guests, who came as a friend and remained a friend throughout his life, was Joseph Haydn. The association between Haydn and Mozart can only be compared with the friendship between Goethe and Schiller. Haydn, considerably older than Mozart, played the rôle of adviser, teacher and father confessor. It is a tribute to the greatness of both that the younger had no reservations about benefiting from the experience of the elder, and that the elder — this is particularly unusual — was no less delighted to be a 'pupil' of the younger.

In 1781, with his Russian Quartets, Joseph Haydn had succeeded in attaining the style which is now called 'classical'. Mozart, gripped by these works, took up the idea and developed it further in a series of six quartets which he completed in 1785 and dedicated to Haydn. The actual phraseology of the dedication he appended to these 'fruits of a long and difficult period of work' are an expression of a deeply felt and sensitive friendship. Haydn acknowledged it, for his part, when he dedicated various pieces of his own later works to Wolfgang Amadeus Mozart.

Joseph Haydn's praise and recognition were a satisfaction not only to himself but also, possibly even more, to his father. In February 1785, Leopold Mozart came to Vienna. The complete reconciliation which had somehow proved impossible in Salzburg was achieved in the capital. Moreover, Leopold had the extreme gratification of hearing Haydn say: 'I tell you before God and as a man of honour that your son is the greatest composer whom I know either per-

Der Schauspieldirektor, a humorous parody, entertained the noble guests gathered in the Orangery Theatre of the Palace of Schönbrunn

sonally or by reputation; he has not only taste but a great skill in composition.'

This was the last great joy that Leopold Mozart was to experience. Happy and contented, he was repaid for all the dark hours which worry over his son had caused him by the joys of these final weeks in Vienna. He spoke no word of reproach, but praised Wolfgang's 'fine lodgings with all the decoration belonging to the house', expressed due appreciation of the prevailing domestic economy, and enjoyed the company of his grandson Karl, born in 1784, besides the various concerts, parties and marks of admiration with which Wolfgang was favoured. The tears stood in his eyes 'for pleasure' when he heard his son playing the piano concerto he had written for Maria Theresia Paradis. He even enjoyed the festive meals of roast pheasant, oysters and coffee at Stephanie's and tolerated his son's mother-in-law.

Such omens seemed to herald a period of sweetness and promise. All Mozart's work of this period, including piano sonatas, chamber music and songs, seems to breathe the contentment he was feeling. He also fostered hopes of an opera.

Figaro
in Mozart's
list of works

Nancy Storace,
the first Susanna

Lorenzo da Ponte

Michael Kelly

After Goldoni's *Lo Sposo Deluso* had had to be dropped while he was still in Salzburg, Mozart had made a special effort, feverishly reading, to find some new material for an opera. A happy chance had thrown him into the path of Lorenzo da Ponte, half-genius, half-adventurer, who swiftly acquired a reputation in Vienna. Mozart suggested that he should adapt a French comedy whose wit and revolutionary satire had already aroused much interest. This was Beaumarchais' *Le Mariage de Figaro*. It fascinated Mozart, and not only on account of its suitability for the stage. The revolutionary plot in which not the master but the man was the centre of all the activity was most tempting. Da Ponte's extremely skilled libretto retained all the pungency of the play and Mozart's music added beauty, point, greatness and mellow humour to the satire.

This relief, on which many copies
were based, is halfway
between reality and idealisation

Was this opera a belated revenge on
Mozart's part for the humiliating
and abusive treatment he had received when he himself served the
Salzburg nobility?

But before *Figaro* could be dealt
with he had an imperial commission to fulfil. There was a small
festival in honour of the governor
of the Netherlands on 7th February
1786, in the Orangery Theatre at
Schönbrunn Palace. Salieri contributed the opera *Prima la musica e
poi le parole* with Italian singers.
Mozart presented the witty pas-
tiche *Der Schauspieldirektor* ('The
Impressario'), with a German cast.
It is only recently that this little
opera has again been produced in its original version, and even today it seems
perfectly apposite to the theatre as we know it. Stephanie spiced the satire
with every possible sarcastic comment on stage manners.

Figaro   But in general the day of opera with spoken dialogue was over. The Italian
opera, which had been re-started in 1783, was gaining the upper hand. So it was
very suitable that Mozart, despite all the myriad difficulties which he experienced, should make his début with an Italian opera, *Le Nozze di Figaro*
Although the performance of Beaumarchais' play was forbidden by the Emperor, he gave his permission for the opera to be rehearsed and performed. On
1st May 1786, its triumphant success silenced its loudest opponents.

Michael Kelly, the Basilio of the first performance, gives an impressive account of it:

'All the original performers had the advantage of the instruction of the

Like the theme of Beethoven's Fifth Symphony, the beginning of Mozart's *Eine kleine Nachtmusik* has become symbolic

composer, who transfused into their minds his inspired meaning. I never shall forget his little animated countenance, when lighted up with the glowing rays of genius; it is as impossible to describe it, as it would be to paint sun-beams. I remember at the first rehearsal of the full band, Mozart was on the stage with his crimson pelisse and gold-laced cocked hat, giving the time of the music to the orchestra. Figaro's song "Non piu andrai", Bennuci gave, with the greatest animation, and power of voice.

I was standing close to Mozart, who, *sotto voce*, was repeating, "Bravo! Bravo! Bennuci", and when Bennuci came to the fine passage, "Cherubino, alla vittoria, alla gloria militar", which he gave out with stentorian lungs, the effect was electricity itself, for the whole of the performers on the stage, and those in the orchestra, as if actuated by one feeling of delight, vociferated "Bravo! Bravo! Maestro — Viva! viva! grande Mozart!" Those in the orchestra I thought would never have ceased applauding, by beating the bows of their violins against the music desks. The little man acknowledged by repeated obeisances, his thanks for the distinguished mark of enthusiastic applause bestowed upon him.'

It might have been expected that after this great success Mozart's fortune would have been made, that his life would have taken a new and happier turn. Nothing of the sort happened. Concerts and tuition remained his only sources of income, just as before. Wolfgang Amadeus Mozart, the opera composer, was an interesting personality but one of purely Viennese interest; and even in Vienna he aroused little excitement. So what was more natural than that Mozart should lose heart and toy with the idea of emigrating to England?

Even his fellow-musicians did not make things over-easy for Mozart. It was admitted that he had a 'decided aptitude for the difficult and unusual'. It is

Leopold Mozart's death certificate

easy to see, looking back from the present, how his 'penetrating brain' would have prevented his direct contact with the world around him. So it was that from this time onward, despite his many friendships, Mozart started to become lonely. Each of the works of this period, the chamber music, the symphony, the essentially classical Eine Kleine Nachtmusik of the summer of 1787, represents an independent whole, complete in itself. And each one is far superior to the usual 'mass production' of the day, from which Mozart had not been able to free himself entirely in his Italian days or even as a fully-fledged musician in Salzburg.

His joy at the triumph with which *Figaro* was hailed in Prague was a ray of light penetrating his general gloom and frustration. *Figaro* was sung, whistled and played by the people of Prague in the streets and the parks, at concerts and at dances. And, when Mozart went to the city for the first time in January 1787, he was commissioned to write another opera.

'Bertramka', the house where the last pages of *Don Giovanni* were written, is situated in the heart of the vineyards of Smichow

After this, Vienna, where others occupied the place in the sun, must have seemed all the more cold and lonely. Bad news from Salzburg hinted that Leopold was near his death. When Mozart at this time quoted from Moses Mendelssohn's *Phaidon* the famous description of death as 'the goal of this life' and a 'friend to man', it was not merely in a transport of emotion. It had long formed the basis of his personal philosophy.

Josepha Duschek

On 28th May 1787 Leopold Mozart died in Salzburg.

The sad news seemed to carry Mozart back to his youth. It comes as a shock to read the two letters which he wrote to his sister at this time. One gets the impression from them that he was so preoccupied with himself and his own worries that he was incapable of expressing any feeling but a prosaic enquiry as to his father's will. From then on his links with Nannerl seemed to be loosened too. It seems as though Mozart was so overwhelmed by everything happening round him that he lost his sense of proportion. Just as, so Lange tells us, he worked off his intense concentration, when he was writing, in a series of nonsensical jokes and pranks, so he hid his sorrow under the curiously inappropriate mask of dispassion and reserve.

In the late summer of 1787, Mozart once again went to Prague — a journey described by the German writer, Mörike, in a charming short novel, *Mozart's Journey to Prague*. Lorenzo da Ponte had completed the libretto for *Don Giovanni* — with the aid of much tobacco and Tokay — in June. He took the theme from the old Spanish tale which goes back as far as Tirso de Molina and had been used again and again by a multitude of different authors — Molière among them. It was now as a *dramma giocoso* to inspire the last great work in the baroque spirit. But instead of a *dramma giocoso* Mozart's work emerged as a tragi-comic masterpiece on the theme of the 'rogue punished', in which gaiety and deep feeling were so intricately mingled that the result never fails to grip an audience, whether played sentimentally, as it was preferred in the last century, or drily, as is the present fashion.

Prague

Franz Xavier Duschek

Mozart had found lodgings for himself in Prague in the Kohlmarkt. Da Ponte lived temporarily in the inn opposite. Legend has it that the two carried on lively conversations out of their windows and across the street. But Mozart felt at his best in a country house which is intimately connected with the story of the completion of *Don Giovanni*. 'Bertramka', belonging to the Duscheks, stood outside the city at the foot

Casanova

Teresa Saporiti

of the vineyards of Smichow. Mozart had known the easily roused Josepha Duschek in Salzburg. Leopold Mozart did not care for her either as a singer or as a person.

There were many stories, anecdotes and rumours about this period, reaching out from the Duschek house to the world outside. Mozart worked with a fiery vehemence and also took a hand at the rehearsals as he had done with *Idomeneo* in Munich. He made various alterations and improvements. He taught Caterina Bondini how to scream during Don Giovanni's unsuccessful seduction, by drastic but efficacious means. He listened to the singers' wishes and satisfied them. The anecdote about the writing of the overture is, however, a charming fantasy. The story goes that he wrote it in its entirety the night before the first performance, while Constanze read to him, and that the musicians played it at sight the next day from the still wet parts. The truth is a little less sensational. The overture was in fact committed to paper in one night but the night before the dress rehearsal; and in any case Mozart's methods of working were such that he planned out an entire work in his head before noting any of it down, so that the actual writing could be completed in an unbroken flow, almost without a pause. The Kegelstatt Trio was written in exactly the same way. The young composer Adalbert Gyrowetz, whom Mozart thought highly of, told a similar story, to the effect that Mozart once wrote a song for a private concert in the adjoining room immediately before it was performed. Again, he improvised the left hand of the Coronation Concerto,

The playbill for the first performance of *Don Giovanni*

written in Prague, without using any written part whatsoever. And it happened on certain occasions that Mozart played his entire piano part from a blank sheet. Feats of this kind were, of course, only possible when Mozart was the performer. He worked on *Don Giovanni* with the greatest concentration and deliberation, completely oblivious of the events taking place around him. But in a letter which he wrote in instalments to Jacquin from Prague he complained of the excessive claims made on him by the outside world: 'for I belong too much to others, and too little to myself; that this is hardly my favourite kind of existence, I do not need to tell you.'

The first performance, arranged for 14th October, had to be postponed until the 29th. The work was staged at last 'with the loudest applause', together with the 'evviva Mozart' which Guardasoni, the director of the Nostitz Theatre, added to the 'evviva da Ponte' in his letters to the equally admired librettist. 'The opera by the great master, Mozart, which we have awaited with such anticipation', was extolled to the heights in the local Prague newspaper: 'musicians and artists say that the like has never yet been produced in Prague. Herr Mozart himself

Rough draft by Casanova for *Don Giovanni*

For inexplicable reasons
Mozart's last symphony
has acquired the
nickname of 'Jupiter'

Doris Stock,
Theodor Körner's aunt,
drew the last portrait of Mozart

conducted and when he entered the orchestra pit he was hailed with three times three. The opera is extremely difficult to execute and every spectator must be amazed at the high standard of the performance after such a short period of rehearsal. Everybody, both singers and players, did their utmost to repay Mozart with a good performance.'

In the audience at this performance was Casanova, the celebrated *picaro* and adventurer, who frequented the Duscheks' house and was a friend of the theatrical director, Bondini. His draft text for a scene in *Don Giovanni* shows that he was acquainted with the theme, so closely reminiscent of his own character and life. It is not known whether he met Mozart at his period.

Figaro and *Don Giovanni* in Prague — these provided the high points of Mozart's life, the few moments of unalloyed happiness when he could forget his ever-increasing difficulties and solitude.

But the success in Prague did nothing to alter his position in Vienna. On 15th November 1787 Gluck died; on 7th December Mozart was appointed 'Imperial Composer' in his place, with half the salary which Gluck had received. Nevertheless the laborious, exhausting tenor of his day-to-day life continued as before. The subscription concerts arranged for June had to be postponed and in the end never took place. In June 1788, deeply engulfed in debts or worries, Mozart wrote the first of his heart-rending begging letters to his fellow Freemason Puchberg: 'Your true friendship and motherly love give me the courage to ask you a great favour: I still owe you eight ducats — besides the fact that I am not in a position to repay them, my trust in you is so great that I dare to ask you to assist me with a further 100 florins until next week (when my academy lessons start in the Casino): then I shall be bound to have my subscription money and will be easily able to pay you back 136 florins with my warmest thanks...'

Mozart's optimism was mere self-deception. The first begging letter was followed by a second and a third — in all more than ten between this date and 1790.

The indifference with which even skilled musicians treated Mozart by remaining away from the Vienna première of *Don Giovanni* in 1788, along with all the other unfortunate circumstances, shows the inability of Mozart's contemporaries to follow his artistic lead. From now on, when true solitude

Mozart at thirty-three

In 1789 Mozart played in St Thomas's Church in Leipzig

The Leipzig Gewandhaus

In Potsdam Mozart took lodgings at the 'Bassin'

began to overshadow his life, his being entered a new phase, took on a new character which was to culminate in the revolutionary outlook of Beethoven.

With only a few exceptions, the works of Mozart's last years were no longer specifically adressed to any particular recipient or recipients. This significantly includes the three famous symphonies of the summer of 1788 with which he concluded his symphonic work — symphonies which he was forced to write independently of any commission or performance. The unrest and insecurity with which his childhood had been filled were repeated at the end of his life. But whereas, when he was a child, these feelings had been alleviated by hope and light-heartedness, now there was only hopelessness and depression. His urge for freedom was, as much as anything, a flight from care.

In April 1789 Mozart precipitately entered on a journey northwards with his pupil Carl von Lichnowsky. They travelled via Prague to Dresden where Doris Stock drew the last portrait of Mozart in the house of Christian Gottfried Körner. Doris Stock, the daughter of a Leipzig engraver, was Körner's sister-in-law and Mozart's aquaintance with her was due to Josepha Duschek. In Dresden there were also concerts and a contest in organ and piano playing with Johann Wil-

helm Hässler, the pupil of a pupil
of Bach's. It was Mozart's last direct contact with the traditions of
the great Bach.

The world of Bach was brought
home to him, too, when he sat at
the organ of St Thomas's Church
(Bach's old church) in Leipzig.
Bach's pupil, Johann Friedrich
Doles, the precentor of the church,
was said by a spectator almost to
have believed that he saw 'his old
master, Sebastian Bach, arisen
again'. In Mozart's honour the
choir sang Bach's motet *Singet dem
Herren* and Mozart himself became
engrossed in Bach's art, overwhelmed with joy at 'work from which
one can really learn something'.

Mozart's last opera buffa, was performed at
the old Burgtheater *(far right)* in the Michaeler Platz

Taking the same route which Bach had once taken to visit his son Carl Philipp
Emanuel at Potsdam, Mozart made for the Prussian imperial residence. Frederick William II, always fond of music, greeted him more kindly than his fellow
musicians. Apart from a few private engagements there was nothing of particular interest to detain him so he decided to return to Leipzig. A concert in
the old Gewandhaus, whose structure was almost imperilled by the volume
Mozart succeeded in drawing from the rather elderly orchestra, brought him
much success but little money.

Perhaps it was because he still cherished a vague hope that the Prussian Court
would respond that he felt impelled to undertake a new journey across
the Elbe. This time Berlin was the goal. He arrived at just the right moment to hear his *Seraglio* being performed at the theatre in the Gendarmenmarkt. According to legend he was refused entry on account of this travelling
clothes, because nobody recognised the small stranger. He soon became known,
however, when he gave vent to his approval and disapproval during the performance. In his short novel *Musikalische Leiden und Freuden* Tieck tells of a
'layman' for whom Mozart's work was the driving force of his youth. This
'layman' was Tieck himself who actually spoke to Mozart during this performance while he was still a schoolboy — the crucial experience of his youth.

The enthusiasm of the Berlin audiences, his joy at unexpectedly meeting his pupil Johann Nepomuk Hummel again and the intelligent benevolence of the king put Mozart in a happy mood. Moreover, a royal commission for six quartets — of which in fact only three were completed — and a concert at Court brought him both money and renewed hope.

The unfortunate situation at Vienna remained unchanged. Mozart's financial position deteriorated yet further when Constanze became ill and had to go to Baden for a cure which increased his debts, despite the money he had earned at Berlin. But just in the nick of time the Emperor remembered his composer and commissioned him to write the opera *Così fan tutte ossia la scuola degli amanti* ('Thus do all Women, or the School for Lovers'). The first performance of this famous work (the libretto was again by da Ponte) took place in the old theatre 'near the castle' on 26th January 1790.

'It is enough, I think, to say of the music that it is by Mozart,' said a newspaper report. In fact da Ponte's witty libretto and Mozart's ironical but deeply felt music were not appreciated to the full either in his own century or the next, when the opera was taken literally and pronounced 'improbable' on account of its immensely complicated plot satirising the inanities current at that time. In it one can foresee the warmth of the clarinet quintet and the great chamber music, the spirit of Mozart's last and greatest mature period. It reveals his heaviness of heart, his awareness of the dark side of life. But mingled with the sadness is the gaiety, the 'hilaritas' characteristic of Mozart. In the midst of all his cares and anxietes he wrote various minuets and the German Dances.

On 20th February 1790 Emperor Joseph II died. This not only marked a break in the political and, even more, the intellectual, life of the day; it was also bound to affect Mozart in one way or another. Could it bring about a change for the better?

'I am now standing on the threshold of good fortune — if I cannot put it to good purpose this time I shall lose it for ever.' Attempting to 'put it to good purpose', he submitted a formal petition. It remained unanswered. Nevertheless, in the general change-over, his prospects seemed not unfavourable. Salieri, of whom the new Emperor thought little, retired from his position as director of the opera. Dismissals were a daily occurrence. But nothing happened to Mozart, either good or bad. He retained his post but his desire for a place as

Per Poſta, S. T. Herr Graf von Szabray, Gouverneur von Fiume, ſ. 4. log. im weiß Lam. Per Poſta, Tit. Herr von Blojer, K. Ung Hofrath, ſ. 3. log. im goldenen Bärn. Den 25 Per Poſta, Herr Mozart, Kön. Ung. Kapellmeiſter, ſ. 2. log. im weiß. Lamm. Per Poſta, Hr. Fink, öſterreichiſcher Courier, paß. durch. Per Poſta, Se. Durchl. Herzog von Garaffa, ſ. 6. paß. durch.

In Regensburg Mozart stayed at the 'Weisses Lamm'

conductor with opportunities for teaching and new commissions remained unfulfilled. Leopold III in his indifference went so far as not to commission a piece from his Imperial Composer for the festivities at the coronation in Frankfurt.

So Mozart, who in any case had almost no pupils and hence nothing to keep him in Vienna, took the desperate step of going to the Frankfurt festivities at his own cost. Together with his brother-in-law, Franz de Paula Hofer, he set out, an uninvited guest, at the end of September 1790.

The journey took him through Regensburg, Nuremberg ('an ugly town'), Würzburg ('a fine, noble town') and Aschaffenburg. It is worth noting as a curiosity that, although he did not know it, one of his most enthusiastic admirers lived in Regensburg — Georg Nikolaus Nissen, who later wrote his biography, and married his widow. An interesting by-product of the journey were Mozart's very varied comments on Nuremberg and Würzburg as he passed through them. From these it is clear that, despite his timeless musical qualities, he was nearer in his tastes to the artistic standpoint of the baroque age than to the new enthusiasm for the Gothic; not surprisingly since this vogue had only recently

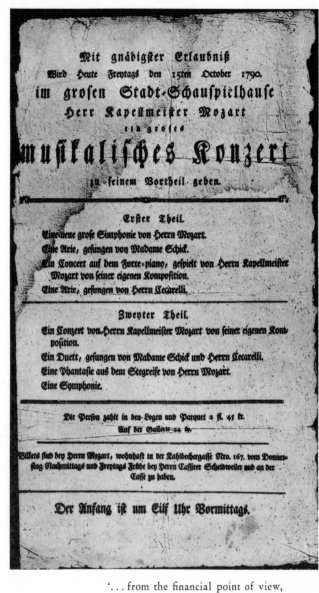

'...from the financial point of view, not successful...' wrote Mozart from Frankfurt of the concert advertised here

been started by Goethe although it was soon to be important in the literary, artistic and historical life of the new romantic era.

Mozart's optimism was quenched when he reached Frankfurt. He was invited and welcomed by many, both the gentry generally and his own old friends, but the coronation hullabaloo awoke more interest than the concert

A meeting between two eras:
the young Kleist was among the
audience at a performance
of *Don Giovanni* at Prague in 1791

he gave, which was 'splendid from the point of view of reputation, but meagre where money is concerned'. He gave another concert with Beecké with whom he had once played in Munich. Perhaps he may have thought of Telemann when he played on the latter's organ in St Katharine's Church. And he visited the André family in Offenbach.

On the way home he passed through Mainz and stopped at Mannheim where the doorkeeper refused to let him enter a rehearsal of *Figaro* because he took him for a tailor's apprentice. In Munich he found the son of Albert, the old innkeeper, and the Electoral Court invited Mozart to perform a concert as a celebration for the visit of the King of Naples; in Vienna they excluded him from the presence of the royal guest. There was the old enthusiasm for Mozart in Munich. He thirsted to stay where he had been so often drawn in vain.

His growing fame was in curious contrast to his penurious life. The older he became the more he was suffocated by poverty. Today it seems incomprehensible. But two centuries ago there was no law of copyright entitling a composer to a reasonable percentage of money earned by his works; nor was there any penalty for pirating another composer's music.

On 15th December, Joseph Haydn left for London and Mozart was alone. Constanze's health remained delicate and her own experiments in dosing herself irritating. His money transactions continued to be unfortunate, and

With *La Clemenza di Tito*
Mozart took his leave of Prague
and Italian opera

LA CLEMENZA
DI TITO,

DRAMMA SERIO PER MUSICA

IN DUE ATTI

DA RAPPRESENTARSI

NEL TEATRO NAZIONALE
DI PRAGA

NEL SETTEMBRE 1791.

IN OCCASIONE DI SOLLENIZZARE

IL GIORNO DELL' INCORONAZIONE

DI SUA

MAESTA L'IMPERATORE
LEOPOLDO II.

NELLA STAMPERIA DI NOB. DE SCHÖNFELD.

the ruinous rates of interest charged him certainly did not improve matters. It is amazing that Mozart did not lose heart altogether, but even more amazing that during these last years his creativity reached its height. He ended his days in the Klein-Kaiserstein house in the Rauhensteingasse to which he had moved from his lodgings in the 'Madonna' in the Judenplatz in 1790. On 4th March 1791 he played his last piano concerto.

In the same month his old friend Schikaneder, who had been principal of the Freihaus Theatre for two years, discussed the possibility of his writing a new fantasy-opera for the theatre. The idea grew into *The Magic Flute*. While Mozart was working on it, at first hesitantly and then with mounting enthusiasm, he was given the commission to write the Requiem which so mystified many of his later biographers. Lorenzo da Ponte too tried to tempt him with plans for an opera in London.

Despite all this activity, he found time to write the Ave Verum, destined not for any particular Court or cathedral but simply for the schoolmaster Stoll and his parish church in Baden.

His current work was interrupted by the completely unexpected request of the Emperor for an opera for the celebration of the coronation of the King of Bohemia in Prague. Caterino Mazzola had prepared a libretto from Metastasio's work *La Clemenza di Tito*. Mozart had to disguise himself, as

Josefa Hofer

it were, in a fashion which had long since been discarded. In the end he paid for this departure from his artistic principles.

With his pupil Süssmayr and Constanze he made a last journey to Prague. *Don Giovanni,* which he conducted, reminded him of happier days. In the audience sat the fourteen-year-old Heinrich von Kleist, later to become a famous German novelist and dramatist: a symbolic meeting of two generations.

The first performance of *La Clemenza di Tito* was no less symbolic: it had only a feeble success. The Empress' description — 'porcheria tedesca' ('German piggery') says more than all the reasoned criticisms. The company which Mozart had tried to please gave frank expression to its dislike through sheer misunderstanding. Mozart was forced to abandon his last hopes and with them all sense of belonging to a period which was by now entirely alien to him.

His departure from Prague was distressing. Perhaps Mozart, already sickly and overworked, really saw in the 'grey messenger', who reminded him of his promise to write the Requiem, a messenger of death. (We know today that the facts were quite simple: the man ordering the requiem was Count Franz von Walsegg-Stuppach, a great music-lover, who looked on it as a sort of party game to present his guests with anonymous compositions. The messenger who gave him this commission for a requiem to be sung at the funeral of the count's wife was the mayor's son, Anton Leitgeb.)

As soon as he returned home Mozart, who since 9th May had been acting as unpaid assistant to the precentor of the cathedral, Hoffmann, continued with his work on *The Magic Flute.* Many stories were circulated concerning carouses organized by Schikaneder and his friends to keep their composer in good spirits. Piece by piece the new opera was written, sometimes in Josephsdorf, sometimes in a pavilion near the Freihaus. It introduced Mozart to a new world, combining the popular theatre and fantasy-drama; he was no longer restricted to the traditions and limitations of Court drama.

The Magic Flute

The 'German opera' had as its theme a fairy tale. Emanuel Schikaneder, whose authorship was later disputed — it was claimed by Karl Ludwig Giseke, an actor and mineralogist — had, with great knowledge of the theatre, concocted a sturdy piece combining both greatness and simplicity. The text, long unjustly depreciated, although Goethe defended it with much insight, became at last nothing less than an ennobled representation in poetic form of humanist ideas and as such it is closely related to such plays as Goethe's *Iphigenie in Aulis* and Schiller's *Don Carlos*. The noble man, Tamino, undergoes various tests in order to achieve wisdom and tells the 'everyday' man, Papageno (a descendant of the comic figure, Staberl, from the old German comedies) to try to conquer his faults. The basic idea of the interrelationship of the noble master and the earthy, common-sensible, though rather ignoble man, is one common to most of European literature from the early Spanish novels to Molière's *Don Juan*; but here it is given weight by Herder's humanistic philosophy and dramatic power and an almost classical though simple form, immeasurably superior to that of the run-of-the-mill 'popular play' of the time. These were the qualities by right of which *The Magic Flute* obtained its prominent place in the history of European culture.

Anna Gottlieb

Not to exaggerate, however, one must admit that the opera would hardly be considered in this light if it were not for Mozart's music. It is, in a sense, his most classical work; in other words, it is the work in which he best succeeds in mingling the native folk music of his country (the enthusiasm for folk music was at its peak at this time) with the highly skilled and refined product of the Courts — the whole being bound together with the greatest artistry of a kind peculiar to Mozart.

If one should wish to name one piece which sums up the whole of Mozart's life, the 'Song of the Two Armed Men' from *The Magic Flute* is probably the most suitable. It represents his final, definitive scheme of creation, and it is no accident that it is obviously influenced by his study of Bach and of Handel whom he knew intimately, having arranged some of his work. In the Requiem this new feeling was confirmed by a new musical language.

On 28th September the composition of *The Magic Flute* was completed with the writing of the overture. Two days later the whole work was performed for the first time. Mozart conducted 'from respect for the gracious and illustrious audience and friendship for the writer of the piece'. The caution with which it was at first greeted was transformed into sheer rejoicing. The enthusiasm grew with every performance. 'But what pleases me most is the silent applause.'

Mozart was in a contented frame of mind. This can be seen from his letters to Constanze, who was again taking the waters at Baden. He took pleasure in drinking his 'black coffee' and smoking his 'splendid pipe of tobacco'. He was even in a mood for practical jokes. At one performance he terrified Schikaneder who was playing Papageno: 'Then I went on stage during Papageno's aria with the glockenspiel, because today I felt an urge to play it myself; I sprang a surprise on Schikaneder by playing an arpeggio when he came to a rest — he started — looked into the wings and saw me — when the place came again I did not play — he stopped and did not want to go on — I guessed what he was thinking and played another chord — then he struck his glockenspiel and said "Shut up!" Everybody laughed — I think that from this joke many people realised for the first time that he was not playing the instrument himself.'

But the deterioration of his health which had already been noticeable in Prague could no longer be impeded. His work on the Requiem cost him enormous trouble. Constanze tried to restore him with walks and conversation and for a while his depression disappeared. But he could no longer throw off his preoccupation with death. The clarinet concerto he wrote for Anton Stadler was his last great work.

His repeated bouts of illness forced them to take medical advice. Mozart's presentiments of death were shot through with an unhealthy fear of having been poisoned. In a letter written in September, presumably to da Ponte, he called the Requiem his *canto funebre*, his swan song, which had yet to be finished. There was no more talk of travelling, either to London or anywhere else. (Although Mozart did not know it Rasumowsky had entered into a correspondence with Prince Potemkin concerning an invitation to Mozart to visit St Petersburg.) All that had become senseless and feeble, like the greater or lesser luxuries in which he had once been interested, such as the ponies that had been his delight.

His last completed work was written on 15th November 1791; it was Schikaneder's masonic cantata, *Laut verkündet unsre Freude* (with the final chorus so much discussed by later commentators — 'Brothers, join your hands in union'). His conducting of this was his last public appearance.

A few days later his condition deteriorated. His sick-bed became a death-bed. The help from the outside world — subscriptions from Holland and Hungary — which was offered as both tribute to his greatness as an artist and sympathy with his frailty as a man, came too late.

Supported by Süssmayr, Mozart continued to work on the Requiem. Benedikt Schack, the first Tamino in *The Magic Flute*, tells how he, Mozart's mother-in-law, Hofer, and the bass, Gerl, who had played Sarastro, sat round Mozart's bed and sang parts of the Requiem, and how suddenly Mozart burst into bitter tears.

Im Jullius.

Die Zauberflöte. — aufgeführt den 30.ten September.
— eine Teutsche Oper in 2 Aufzügen von Eman. Schikaneder.
bestehend in 22 Stücken. — Hauptpersonen. — Mad.elle Gottlieb. Mad.me Hofer. Mad.e Görl.
Mad.elle Klöpfler. Mad.elle Hofmann. Männer. Hr. Schack. Hr. Görl. Hr. Schikaneder der ältere.
Hr. Kistler. Hr. Schikaneder der jüngere. Hr. Nouseul. — Chör.

Den 5.ten September. — aufgeführt in Prag den 6.ten September.
La Clemenza di Tito opera seria in Due Atti per l'incoro-
nazione di sua maestà l'imperatore Leopoldo II. — ridotta à
vera opera dal Sig.re Mazzolà. Poeta di sua A: S: l'Elettore di
Sassonia. — Attrici: — Sig.ra Marchetti fantozzi. — Sig.ra Antonini.
— Attori. Sig.re Bedini. Sig.re Carolina Perini /da uomo/ Sig.re
Baglioni. Sig.re Campi. — e Cori. — 24 Pezzi.

Den 28.ten September.
Zur Oper, die Zauberflöte — einen Priestermarsch und die Ouverture.

Ein Konzert für die Clarinette. für Hrn. Stadler den ältern.
Begleitung. 2 violni, viola, 2 flauti, 2 fagotti, 2 Corni e Bassi.

Den 15.ten November.

Eine kleine Freymaurer = Kantate. bestehend aus 1 Chor. 1 Aria.
2 Recitativen, und ein Duo. Tenor und Bass.
2 violini, viola, Basso; 1 flauto, 2 obe e 2 Corni. —

In the last year of his life, Mozart had few entries to make in the record he kept of his works

Finale   With a clear mind he saw his end approaching yet still felt himself to be one with his fellow men. While his body was sinking his still active thoughts were with *The Magic Flute*, mentally taking part in all that was going on in the theatre.

Thirty years later Sophie Haibl, Constanze's sister, told how she was met by Constanze when hurrying, full of premonitions, down the Rauhensteingasse. 'How I started when I saw my sister, half desperate and yet still trying to control herself, coming towards me. She said: "Thank God, Sophie, that you are here. Tonight he is so ill that I am afraid that he will not survive until tomorrow." I tried hard to collect myself and went to his bedside where he immediately called out to me: "Thank goodness you have come, Sophie. You must see me die." I tried to fortify myself and talk him out of it; but he only went on replying to everything: "I already have the taste of death in my mouth." Lord, how desperate I felt. My poor sister followed me out and begged me for God's sake to go to the Brothers of St Peter's and ask one of them to come as quickly as possible. I did so, alone . . . they hesitated for a long time and it took me a great deal of trouble to persuade one of these Brothers to come . . .'

When Sophie returned, Süssmayer was sitting with Mozart. 'On the bed lay the famous Requiem and Mozart was telling him how he wanted him to finish it after his death. Moreover he charged his wife to keep his death a secret until she should have informed Albrechtsberger, for the task of proclaiming his

Shaken by the news of Mozart's death, Haydn wrote only these few words in his diary

Constanze's dirge in Dr Sigismund Barisani's album – directly under a few lines in Mozart's hand

Mozart died in the first storey of the Kaltersteins' house, where, a few months earlier, his youngest son had been born

death was pre-eminently his. People searched for the Doctor, Closett, and found him eventually in the theatre; but he insisted on waiting until the play was over. Then he came and ordered further cold bandages for Mozart's still burning head; these shocked him so much that he did not recover before he expired.'

Mozart died at five minutes to two during the night of 5th December. The Requiem remained incomplete. It breaks off with the ninth bar of the Lacrimosa.

Mozart's illness, which is only now being systematically analysed and is still matter for discussion, gave rise to many legends and stories. There was talk of poisoning. Salieri was named and various other potential murderers. But Mozart was killed by his misuse of his physical powers, which had been grossly overtaxed ever since his earliest youth, and by his mental suffering, which deprived him of the will to live.

It is curious that the death of Mozart, the embodiment of frankness and clarity, both as a man and an artist, should have been surrounded by mystery and complication.

On the advice of Gottfried van Swieten, Constanze, overwhelmed by sorrow and illness and incapable of making any decisions, arranged a miserable

Mozart's last composition

funeral at the lowest possible cost. She herself was with friends when the
black-shrouded corpse was borne out of the house in the afternoon of 6th December. The procession stopped for benediction on the north side of St
Stephen's at the chapel of the Holy Cross. A few friends, among them van
Swieten, Salieri and Süssmayer, accompanied the cortège as far as the door.
What then happened is uncertain. Tradition has it that the cortège turned
back at he door on account of the wet weather and the hearse continued
through the rain followed only by a small dog. Mozart was buried outside the
walls of the city in the Churchyard of St Marx, in a pauper's grave, without
a tombstone or a cross to mark the spot. How and why all this happened
remains a mystery.

Van Swieten's attitude becomes slightly more comprehensible when one
realises that he himself was beset with worries, due to the change of sovereign.
But was it intentional or merely a result of the customs of the day that the
funeral should have been so prosaic and solitary? And then there remains the
contradiction between the generally held belief that there was a storm when
Mozart was buried and a private diary entry which makes no mention of
either rain or snow. Even more remarkable is the fact that it was not until
1808 that Constanze visited the graveyard, induced to do so by Nissen, her
second husband. In the intervening period the grave had become impossible
to find . . .

The place where Mozart is thought to be buried is now marked by a broken
column with an angel in an attitude of mourning.

1756 27th January: Wolfgang Amadeus Mozart was born in 9 Getreidegasse, Salzburg. Baptized in the Cathedral on 28th January. Publication of Leopold Mozart's violin manual and Gessner's *Idyllen*.

1757 Leopold Mozart became Court composer at Salzburg.

1758 Leopold Mozart was promoted to the second desk of the Court orchestra.

1759 Death of Handel. Haydn's first symphony. Lessing's *Faust*. Birth of Schiller.

1760 Beginning of Mozart's musical education (along with his sister Nannerl, born in 1751).

1761 Spring: Mozart's first composition · 1st September: first public appearance as a member of the choir in Eberlin's *Sigismundus Hungariae Rex* in Salzburg.

1762 12th January to beginning of February: Mozart family on tour in Munich · 18th September: began journey to Vienna via Passau and Linz. Birth of Constanze Weber. Rousseau's *Emile* and *Contrat Social*.

1763 5th January: return to Salzburg. Mozart fell ill. First portrait of Mozart · 28th February: Leopold Mozart became deputy conductor in Salzburg · 9th June: departure of family for Paris (arrived on 18th November) · 24th December: Versailles.

1764 9th January: return to Paris. Mozart became ill. Publication of his first printed works, the Piano Sonatas · 10th April: departure for London (arrived 23rd April). Met J. C. Bach. London sketchbook. First symphonies.

1765 14th July: tour to Calais, Dunkirk, Lille (where Mozart and his father became ill), Ghent, Antwerp, The Hague (arrived on 11th November: later fell ill). Violin sonatas, piano works, *Galimathias musicum*.

1766 End of January: journey to Amsterdam · February: return to The Hague. Visit to Scheveningen · April: to Amsterdam via Haarlem · 17th April: to Utrecht and then to Brussels via Rotterdam, Antwerp and Malines · Arrived in Brussels on 8th May · Continued through Valenciennes and Cambrai to Paris (arrived 10th May) · 9th July: journey through Dijon, Lyons to Geneva · 7th September: to Lausanne · 11th September: to Berne · 18th September: through Aargau to Zürich · 4th October: on to Schaffhausen (till 9th October) and Donaueschingen. Return via Messkirch, Ulm, Günzburg, Dillingen, Markt Biberbach, Augsburg, Munich (where he was ill) to Salzburg (arrived 30th November).

1767 12th March: first performance of the oratorio *Die Schuldigkeit des ersten und fürnehmsten Gebottes* in Salzburg. Holy week: *Grabmusik* · 13th May: first performance of his Latin comedy *Apollo et Hyacinthus*. Composed piano concertos (adaptations) and church voluntaries. Painting of the portrait of Mozart by Helbling · 11th September: journey to Vienna (arrived September) · 13th October: journey to Brünn and Olmütz (Mozart and his sister fell ill).

1768 9th January: journey to Vienna (arrived 10th January). July: Mozart completed his first Italian opera *La Finta Semplice*. Composed symphonies, divertimenti, arias, church and chamber music · October: first performance of *Bastien et Bastienne* in Dr Mesmer's house · 8th December: first performance of the Orphanage Mass conducted by Mozart. Violin sonatas, Missa Brevis in D, Symphony in D.

1769 Beginning of January: journey to Salzburg (arrived 5th January) · 1st May: first performance of *La Finta Semplice* in Salzburg · Summer: the first serenades · October: 'Dominicus' Mass in St Peter's, Salzburg · 14th November: Mozart became unpaid Court conductor · 13th December: beginning of the first Italian tour.

1770 Beginning of January: in Verona. Della Rossa painted portrait of Mozart · 10th January: departure for Mantua · 20th January: to Bozzolo, Cremona and Milan (arrived 23rd January). Composed arias · 15th March: journey to Lodi (composed the first string quartet) · 16th March: travelled on through Padua and Modena to Bologna (arrived 24th March) and Florence (arrived 30th March) · 7th April: through Viterbo to Rome (arrived 11th April) · 8th May: departure for Naples · 25th June: return to Rome · 6th July: received in audience by Pope Clement XIV · 10th July: to Bologna (arrived 20th July) · 9th October: honoured by the Accademia Filarmonica. Began to compose the opera *Mitridate, Re di Ponto*. Ecclesiastical compositions · 13th October: via Parma to Milan (arrived

18th October). Mozart received the title of conductor of the Accademia Filarmonica of Verona · 26th December: first performance of *Mitridate* in Milan.

1771 January: short visit to Turin · 4th February: beginning of journey home via Canonica, Venice (11th February—12th March), Padua (commissioned to write the oratorio *La Betulia Liberata*). 28th March: arrival in Salzburg. Commissioned to write the 'azione teatrale' *Ascanio in Alba*, for Milan · 13th August: began the second Italian tour, via Rovereto, Ala, Verona, Brescia to Milan (arrived 21st August). Met Hasse · 17th October: first performance of *Ascanio in Alba* · 5th December: return home via Ala and Bressanone · 16th December: arrival in Salzburg. Death of Prince Bishop Sigismund von Schrattenbach.

1772 14th March: election of Archbishop Hieronymus Colloredo · 29th April: first performance of Mozart's festival opera *Il Sogno di Scipione* in Salzburg. Composed instrumental works (symphonies) · 9th August: Mozart appointed salaried Court conductor · 24th October: beginning of the third Italian tour through Innsbruck to Milan (arrived 4th November) · 26th December: first performance of the opera *Lucio Silla* in Milan. Composed the ballet *La Gelosia del Seraglio*, church and instrumental works (quartets, the motet *Exsultate, Jubilate*).

1773 Beginning of March: return home via Bressanone (arrived 14th March). Family moved into the house of a dancing master in the Hannibalplatz, Salzburg. Composed symphonies, divertimenti, church music · July: departure for Vienna (arrived 16th July) · 5th August: received by Empress Maria Theresa. Composed instrumental music (the Antretter Serenade, quartets, piano music). End of September: return to Salzburg.

1774 Productive period of composition in Salzburg. Began the opera *La Finta Giardiniera* · 6th December: journey to Munich (arrived 8th December).

1775 13th January: first performance of the opera *La Finta Giardiniera* in Munich (Redoutensaal). Composed the 'Sparrow' Mass, wind divertimenti, a bassoon concerto, the Dürrnitz Sonata. Piano contest with Beecke in Albert's house · 6th March: return to Salzburg · 23rd April: first performance of the opera *Il Re Pastore* for Archduke Maximilian Franz in Salzburg. Composed violin concertos, divertimenti and serenades.

1776 Stay in Salzburg. Composed piano concertos, serenades (January: Serenata Notturna; July: Haffner Serenade), divertimenti, church music (December: Organ Solo Mass).

1777 Composed divertimenti, a piano concerto (January), the Notturno for orchestra (January), the Ferlandis Concerto for oboe (summer) · 14th March: asked for permission to travel (refused) · Summer: visit to the Duschek family · 28th August: second application to the archbishop · 1st September: dismissal · 22nd/23rd September: Mozart left Salzburg with his mother · 24th September: arrival in Munich (lodged in the 'Schwarzer Adler', belonging to Albert). Fruitless audiences with the nobility, including Count Seeau and Elector Max Josef III. Albert's plan to provide him with an income (3rd October: concert in the 'Schwarzer Adler'). New plans for Italy · 11th October: departure for Augsburg (stayed in the ,Weisses Lamm'). New friends, the 'little cousin' · 26th October: journey to Hohen-Altheim (mit Beecke again) · 28th October: journeyed on to Mannheim (arrived 30th October). Lived in the 'Pfalzischer

Hof' but moved in December to the Serrarius' house. Worked for the Court of Karl Theodor, met Vogler, Holzbauer, Toeschi, Gemmingen, Wieland, and became friendly with Wendling, Cannabich and the Weber family (in particular Aloysia).

1778 20th February: Mozart became ill · 14th March: left Mannheim · 23rd March: arrived in Paris, came into close contact with Grimm and Le Gros; gave lessons · April: moved to the rue du Gros Chenet · 11th June: first performance of the ballet *Les Petits Riens* · 3rd July: death of Mozart's mother. Mozart moved to the house of Mme d'Epinay. Met J. C. Bach. Composed piano sonatas (including those in A major and A minor) · 9th August: return to Paris · 11th September: end of close association with Grimm · 25th September: journey via Nancy to Strasbourg (concerts) · 3rd November: on to Mannheim (arrived 6th November). Composed the opera *Semiramis* (now lost) to a libretto by Gemmingen · Unsympathetically received by Aloysia Weber.

1779 Beginning of January: the 'little cousin' stayed in Munich · 13th January: returned with the 'little cousin' to Salzburg · 15th January: arrival in Salzburg. Requested the Archbishop to be reinstated · 17th January: appointed Court organist · 23rd March: completed the Coronation Mass. Composed serenades, divertimenti, church music, Symphony in B flat major, completed the music for Gebler's *Thamos*, worked on *Das Serail* by Schachtner.

1780 Composed church and instrumental music. Autumn: first meeting with Schikaneder. Worked on *Idomeneo* · 5th November: departure for Munich (lodged in the Burggasse). Death of Empress Maria Theresa.

1781 Met his father and sister in Munich · 29th January: first performance of *Idomeneo* in the Residenztheater (built by Cuvilliés). Munich carnival. Composed arias, an oboe quartet, the Munich Kyrie · March: travelled to Vienna at the Prince Bishop's request · 16th March: arrived in Vienna. Completed the Munich Serenade for wind instruments. Composed the Horn Rondo and 2 violin sonatas · 2nd May: moved to new quarters · 8th June: final break with the Prince Bishop and end of service for the Salzburg Court · 30th July: began work on *Il Seraglio* · 24th December: played in piano contest with Clementi before Joseph II. Blackmailed by the Weber's mother and Thorwart, became engaged to Constanze Weber. Constanze moved to house of Baroness Waldstätten.

1782 Entertained in Gottfried van Swieten's house. Growth of Baroque in Vienna. Mozart studied the fugue (Bach, Handel) · 26th May: gave his first concert in the Augarten · 16th July: first performance in the Burgtheater of *Il Seraglio*, completed on 29th May · End of July: wind serenade in C · 4th August: married to Constanze Weber.

1783 Subscription edition of his piano concertos. Gave many concerts (Academy on 23rd March). Changes of address (first the Kohlmarkt, then 3 Judenplatz) · 7th May: first meeting with da Ponte · End of May: fell ill. Continued the Mass in C major begun in the summer of 1782 · 17th June: birth of a son, Raimund Leopold · July: began work on the opera *L'Oca del Cairo* (unfinished) · End of July: arrival of Mozart and Constanze in Salzburg. Work on the opera *Lo Sposo Deluso* (unfinished) · 19th August: death in Vienna of Raimund Leopold · 25th August: first performance of the Mass in C minor in St Peter's, Salzburg · 27th

October: return to Vienna via Linz (Linz Symphony).

1784 23rd January: moved to the Trattnerhof in the Graben · February: began making his own list of his works · March: gave concerts at the houses of Galitzin, Zichy, Palffy and in public halls. Composed piano concerto (the Ployer Concerto), sonatas, chamber music. Met Sarti and Paesiello. Fell ill · 21st August: Nannerl married Baron Berchtold von Sonnenburg in St Gilgen · 21st September: birth of Mozart's son, Karl Thomas (died 1856) · October: moved to 8 Schulergasse · 14th December: became member of a masonic lodge.

1785 28th January: Leopold Mozart went via Munich to Vienna (arrived 11th February). Concerts in the Mehlgrube. Met Joseph Haydn. Completed the quartets dedicated to Haydn · 10th March: *Davidde Penitente* was performed. Full social life · 6th April: Leopold Mozart joined his son's masonic lodge · 25th April: Leopold returned home via Munich. Mozart was busy with concerts and compositions (June: the song *Das Veilchen*, chamber music, symphonies) · October, began composing *The Marriage of Figaro*.

1786 Wrote *Der Schauspieldirektor* · 7th February: first performance in Schönbrunn. Became a firm friend of Jacquin. Dittersdorf was in Vienna. Acquired new pupils (including J. N. Hummel) · 1st May: first performance of *Figaro* in the Burgtheater · 18th October: birth of his son Johann Thomas Leopold (died 15th November).

1787 8th January: Mozart left for Prague (arrived 11th January) · 17th January: *Figaro* performed in Prague · February: returned to Vienna · Spring: quintets. Fell ill. Moved to 224 Landstrasse. Took over the direction of the Handel concerts · 28th May: death of his father in Salzburg. Instrumental music (August: Eine kleine Nachtmusik) and songs · 2nd September: death of Dr Barisani. Work on *Don Giovanni* · Beginning of October: went to Prague where he met the Duscheks and Casanova · 29th October: first performance of *Don Giovanni* · 15th November: death of Gluck. Mozart returned to Vienna · 1st December: moved to 281 Tuchlauben · 7th December succeeded Gluck as Royal Court Composer · 27th December: birth of a daughter.

1788 Instrumental music and dances (24th February: Coronation Concerto) · 7th May: *Don Giovanni* in Vienna · 17th June: moved to the 'Drei Sterne' · 29th June: death of his daughter Therese · June–August: the last three symphonies in E flat, G minor, C ('Jupiter').

1789 Moved to the Judenplatz · 4th March: wrote wind parts for Handel's *Messiah* · 7/8th April: Travelled with Lichnowsky via Mährisch-Budweis to Prague (arrived 10th April). Continued to Dresden (arrived 12th April). Stayed in Hotel de Pologne · 14th April: gave concert at Court. Piano and organ contests with J. W. Hässler · 16th April: Doris Stock drew Mozart's last portrait · 18th April: continued journey to Leipzig · 20th April: on to Potsdam (arrived 25th April) · 7th May: returned to Leipzig · 12th May: concert in the Gewandhaus · 17th May: journey to Berlin (arrived 19th May). *Il Seraglio* performed in the theatre in the Gendarmenmarkt (Tieck) · 26th May: concert at the Prussian Court. Commissioned to write the Prussian Quartets · 28th May: left for Prague (arrived 31st May) · 2nd June: continued to Vienna (arrived 4th June). Began work on the Prussian Quartets. Financial position worsened. Constanze in Baden · 29th September: completed

the Clarinet Quintet · October: began to write *Così Fan Tutte* · 16th November: birth and death of his daughter Anna.

1790 26th January: first performance of *Così Fan Tutte* in the Burgtheater · 20th February: death of Emperor Joseph II. Finances worsened still further. Application for post of Court conductor remained unanswered. Süssmayr became Mozart's pupil · June: Mozart with Constanze in Baden. Ill. July: arranged Handel's *Alexander's Feast* and *Ode on St Cecilia's Day*. Friendly with Stoll. Moved to the Rauhensteingasse · 15th December: Haydn left for London. Mozart thought of emigrating to England. String quintets, fantasy for mechanical organ, and first work on *The Magic Flute*.

1791 8th January: completed last piano concerto (in B flat major) · 9th May: became unpaid assistant to Hoffmann, choirmaster of the Cathedral. Wrote songs and dances. Stayed in Baden (4 Renngasse) · 17th June: *Ave verum* · 26th July: birth of a son, Franz Xaver Wolfgang (died 1844) · July: commissioned to write the Requiem and *La Clemenza di Tito* · 15th August: went to Prague with Constanze and Süssmayr · 29th August: *Don Giovanni* in Prague · 6th September: coronation of Leopold II as King of Bohemia. First performance of *La Clemenza di Tito* · Mid-September: return to Vienna. Depressed state of mind · 29th September: completed *The Magic Flute* (30th September: first performance in the Freihaus Theatre, Vienna) · 7th October: finished clarinet concerto · 15th November: last finished composition, *Laut verkündet . . .* · 18th November: first performance of the cantata conducted by Mozart · 20th November: confined to bed · 5th December: died · 6th December: burial in the graveyard of St Marx.

WOLFGANG AMADEUS MOZART in 1780/1. Detail of the family group by Johann Nepomuk della Croce (1736–1819). *Mozarteum, Salzburg*

5 Detail of a letter of 9th February 1756 from Leopold Mozart to the Augsburg publisher, Johann Jakob Lotter, announcing the news of his son's birth. *City Archives, Augsburg*

6 Pfersee near Augsburg in the 18th century

The conferment of civic rights by the town of Augsburg on David Mozart (died 1685) from Pfersee in 1643. *City Archives, Augsburg*

7 Augsburg: view of the town from the west, about 1730. Painting by J. C. Weyermann (1698–1757). *City Collection, Augsburg*

8 The house in St Gilgen where Mozart's mother was born.

9 Leopoldskron: view from the château of the pond on the Untersberg. Leopoldskron was occupied by Franz Lactantius Firmian (1712–1786), a gifted artist himself, who was chief steward at Salzburg and very fond of Mozart. *Photo: Frank*

10 No. 9 Getreidegasse, Salzburg, the house owned by the Hagenauers, where Mozart was born to Leopold and Anna Maria Mozart. After a lithograph by C. Czichna. *Mozarteum, Salzburg*

11 Mozart's mother, Anna Maria Mozart, née Pertl (1720–1778). This painting,

dating from 1775, is probably by Pietro A. Lorenzoni (1721–1786). *Mozarteum, Salzburg*

Leopold Mozart (1719–1787). From an oil-painting of 1770, probably also painted by Pietro Lorenzoni. *Mozarteum, Salzburg*

12 Salzburg in winter. View from the road running below the fortress on to the Cathedral, St Peter's, the Church of the Franciscans and the Residency. *Photo: Stibor*

Entry in the baptismal register of the diocese of Salzburg (1756, page 2), recording the baptism on 28th January 1756 of Johannes Chrysostomus Wolfgangus Theophilus (Theophilus is the hellenized form of Amadeus) in the presence of his godfather Dr Johannes Theophilus Pergmayr, city senator and merchant. *Cathedral Archives, Salzburg.*

13 Court of the house where Mozart was born. View from the corridor of the third floor, directly outside the room in which he was born on to the narrow courtyard. In the background is a tower of the College or University Church designed by Fischer von Erlach. *Photo: Frank*

15 Mozart's first composition written between February and April 1761. *Private collection*

16 Mozart in his 'Court clothes' in about 1762. Probably painted by Pietro Antonio Lorenzoni. *Mozarteum, Salzburg*

17 Marie Antoinette (born 1755). This portrait by F. Wagenschein shows the princess when about seven years old. *Austrian National Library, Vienna*

18 Franz Felix Anton von Mölk (1714–76), Court Chancellor of Salzburg, whose family were among the Mozarts' friends. After a silhouette. *Mozarteum, Salzburg*

Lorenz Hagenauer (1712–1792). Until about 1773 he was the Mozarts' 'landlord'. Anonymous portrait from his tombstone in the St Peter's graveyard, Salzburg. *Mozarteum, Salzburg*

19 Robinig House. *Photo: Frank*

20 Störzer's inn 'Zum Hirschen' in the Theatinerstrasse, Munich, where the Mozarts stayed in 1763. After a watercolour by J. Puschkin, beginning of the 19th century. *City Museum, Munich*

21 Nicolo Jommeli (1714–1774). Anonymous portrait. *Austrian National Library, Vienna*

22 Two of the extant pages from Nannerl's diary of the journey, with entries by Nannerl and her mother. The marginal comments are by Ludwig Nohl (1831–1885), an expert on the lives of Mozart and Beethoven. *Mozarteum, Salzburg*

23 Brussels. View of the town after an engraving by Antonin Cardas, dating from the 18th century. *Austrian National Library, Vienna*

24 Leopold Mozart with his son and daughter. Painted by Louis Carmontelle in 1763 and engraved a year later by Jean Baptiste Delafosse. There is another version, possibly the 'original' one, in in which only the father and son are shown. *Mozarteum, Salzburg*

25 Friedrich Melchior Grimm (1723–1807), known as Baron 'de Grimm', was born in Regensburg but, after completing his studies in Leipzig, lived from 1748 to 1789 in Paris. In 1776 he became minister of Saxe-Gotha at the Court of France. He was a member of Rousseau's circle, one of the leading Encyclopédistes, and a *littérateur* of whom Goethe thought highly. He died in Gotha. This engraving is by Jacques-Nicolas Tardieu (1716–1791). *Historisches Bildarchiv Handke*

Mozart's first printed work, the *Sonate pour le Clavecin* (title-page) containing early piano pieces with violin accompaniment. 'Madame Victoire de France' (1733–1799) was Louis XV's daughter

26 Daines Barrington (1727–1800), an English lawyer, historian, archaeologist and scientist. *Hulton Pictures, London*

Johann Christian Bach (1735–1782), Johann Sebastian's youngest son, went to Milan in 1756, and to London, where he passed the rest of his life, in 1762. The illustration shows the 'London' Bach after a portrait by Thomas Gainsborough. *Liceo Musicale, Bologna*

Extract from the 'London Sketchbook' (1764), in which the phraseology and the childishly wobbly handwriting are Mozart's own. *Former Prussian State Library, Berlin*

27 London. This view over the Thames, was painted by Antonio Canaletto in 1746/7. *Národni Gallery, Prague*

28 The Swan Inn, Cornhill, where Leopold Mozart 'exhibited' his children. *Russ Allan, London*

29 Announcement of a concert by Wolfgang and Nannerl published in the *Public Advertiser* of 11th July 1865.

30 Simon André Tissot (1728–1797), a doctor and psychologist from Lausanne.

31 Geneva in the 18th century. View of the whole town by Linck. *Austrian National Library, Vienna*

32 Dedication by Salomon Gessner (1730–1788). The Swiss poet, painter, publisher and bookseller gave the Mozarts a copy of his complete works published in 1765/6 (by Orell Gessner and Co., Zürich) with a handwritten dedication. *Mozarteum, Salzburg*

33 Salomon Gessner at the age of 36. Oil painting by Anton Graaff (1736–1813). The picture is the property of the Gottfried Keller Society. *Swiss State Museum, Vienna*

34 Michael Haydn (1737–1806). Lithograph by F. Eybl. *Austrian National Museum, Vienna*

Sylvester Barisani (1719–1810). After an oil painting by Johann Nepomuk della Croce. *Mozarteum, Salzburg*

Title-page of the libretto for *Die Schuldigkeit des ersten und fürnehmsten Gebottes*. *Reference Library, Salzburg*

35 Vienna from the Belvedere, after an engraving by Carl Schütz. *Austrian National Library, Vienna*

37 Mozart in 1766/7, a portrait by Thaddäus Helbling, a painter from Salzburg. There are doubts about the authenticity of the picture. *Mozarteum, Salzburg*

38 Christoph Willibald Gluck (1714–1787), anonymous portrait of 1755. *B. Schott and Sons, Mainz*

Pietro Metastasio (1698–1782), after an engraving by Paolo Caronni (after Johann Nepomuk Steiner). *Austrian National Library, Vienna*

39 Organ of the Waisenhauskirche, Vienna, where Mozart conducted the first performance of his Waisenhaus Mass

(K. 47a) on 8th December 1768. *Photo: Hubmann*

40 Pater Dominicus Hagenauer (1746–1811) for whose first service Mozart wrote the Dominicus Mass. A son of Lorenz Hagenauer, he later became Abbot of St Peter's. *Mozarteum, Salzburg*

41 Sigismund Count Schrattenbach (1698–1771) became Prince Bishop of Salzburg in 1753. *Mozarteum, Salzburg*

Mozart's travelling expenses. Entry in the archbishop's own hand in the cashbook of the Privy Purse, 27th November 1769. *Archives, Salzburg*

42 Italy as shown on a map printed in Venice in 1780. *Istituto Italiano di Cultura, Munich*

43 The Baedeker of the 18th century. The Mozarts prepared for their tours of Europe by reading Johann Georg Keyssler's book *Recent Travels* (Hanover 1751). *Deutsche Mozart Gesellschaft, Augsburg*

44 Mozart in 1770. This portrait, painted at the beginning of January in the Lugiati's house in Verona is by either Gian Bettino Cignaroli (1706–1770) or his nephew Saverio della Rossa (1745–1821). The original was in the possession of Alfred Cortot. *Mozarteum, Salzburg*

46 Nicola Piccini (1728–1800), an engraving by Louis Jacques Cathelin after the painting by Charles Jean Robineau. *Austrian National Library, Vienna*

47 Milan in 1730 after a drawing by Friedrich Bernhard Werner. *Austrian National Library, Vienna*

48 Joseph Mysliweczek (1737–1781), 'il Boemo'. Detail of an engraving by A. Widerhafer. *Sváz Ceskoslovenskych Skadatelu, Prague*

49 Padre Martini (1706–1784), after a drawing by Giovanni Rubini. *Mozarteum, Salzburg*

Postscript to a letter (written on 10th February 1770 in Milan) from Leopold Mozart to his wife and daughter. *Mozarteum, Salzburg*

51 Piazza del Popolo, Rome. From Giambattista Piranesi's *Vedute di Roma 1772–1778. Istituto Italiano di Cultura, Munich*

52 Naples in 1782. The fortress of S. Elena and Vesuvius seen from the Molo, after a painting by Alessandro d'Amea. *Austrian National Library, Vienna*

53 The Sistine Chapel. *Austrian National Library, Vienna*

54 The diploma of Mozart's Order. The illustration shows a copy of the diploma in Leopold's hand. *Conservatorio G. B. Martini, Bologna*

55 Pope Clement XIV, 1705–1774 *Austrian National Library, Vienna*

56 Charles Burney (1726–1814), the outstanding English musicologist and composer. A stippled engraving by Francesco Bartolozzi after the painting by Joshua Reynolds. *Austrian National Library, Vienna*

57 Teatro Ducale, Milan, interior, 1747. After an engraving by Marc' Antonio dal Re. *Museum, Milan*

59 Staircase in the dancing-master's house in the Hannibalplatz to which the Mozarts moved in 1773. This staircase led up to the Mozarts' roomy apartments. The Hannibalplatz is now known as the Makartplatz. *Photo: Frank*

60 Archduke Ferdinand of Austria (1754–1806), an engraving by Christian Fritzsch, after the painting by Franz Wagenschein, 1768. *Austrian National Library, Vienna*

61 Johann Adolph Hasse (1699–1783), an engraving by Lorenzo Zucchi after the

painting by Pietro Antonio Rotari. *Austrian National Library, Vienna*

62 Hieronymus Count Colloredo (1732–1812), Prince Bishop of Salzburg from 1772 to 1803, and Salzburg's last overlord. After a portrait by Franz Xaver König, 1772. *Mozarteum, Salzburg*

Ferdinand Count Zeill (1719–1786), Bishop of Chiemsee. *Mozarteum, Salzburg*

63 Barbara von Mölk (1752–1828), daughter of the Court Chancellor of Salzburg. Mozart fell in love with her, and her brother Franz paid court to Nannerl. *Mozarteum, Salzburg*

Sheet of parchment embroidered with silk representing air-gun shooting, the Mozart family's favourite sport. The picture belonged to Leopold Mozart. *Mozarteum, Salzburg*

64 Empress Maria Theresa (1717–1780), wife of Emperor Franz I, after the death of whose son Joseph II became co-regent. After a portrait by Joseph Ducreux, 1769. *Austrian National Library, Vienna*

65 No. 18 Tiefer Graben where the Mozarts stayed when in Vienna in 1773 (probably also in 1768). The house belonged to the Fischers. *Photo: Hubmann*

66 Prannerstrasse, Munich. In the 18th century the Redoutenhaus, later demolished, stood here. On 13th January 1775 it witnessed the first performance of Mozart's *La Finta Giardiniera. City Museum, Munich*

67 Beginning of the Andante Cantabile movement of the Violin Concerto in D Major (K. 218) in Mozart's writing. In the same year, 1775, he also wrote the four violin concertos, K. 207, 211, 216 and 219. *Former Prussian State Library, Berlin*

68/9 Mozart's request for leave of 28th August 1777 (superscription and beginning), with the Archbishop's laconic comment: 'To be sent to the exchequer with the advice that father and son should have permission to seek their fortune elsewhere.'

69 Prince Maximilian Josef III of Bavaria (1727–1777) with a Court official, Count Joseph Anton von Seeau (died 1799), who came into contact with Mozart in Munich. Unfortunately the music-loving prince had no 'vacancy'. Painted by Georg Desmarées (1696–1776), an ancestor of the painter, Hans von Marées. *Residency Museum, Munich*

70 Mozart's 'little cousin', Maria Anna Thekla Mozart (1758–1841), daughter of his uncle, Franz Aloys Mozart. Anonymous pencil-drawing, 1778. *Mozarteum, Salzburg*

71 Mozart wearing his Order. Painted in the autumn of 1777, probably by della Croce. *Mozarteum, Salzburg*

Franz Albert (1728–1789), the 'scholar landlord', who tried to arrange for Mozart to stay in Munich. *City Museum, Munich*

72 Cäcilie Weber, née Stamm (1727–1793), Mozart's mother-in-law and Carl Maria von Weber's aunt. Anonymous silhouette. *Mozarteum, Salzburg*

73 Aloysia Lange, née Weber (c. 1760–1831), Mozart's sweetheart and later his sister-in-law, married Josef Lange (1751–1831) in 1780. From Hieronymus Löschenkohl's *Austrian National Almanach*, 1785. *Mozarteum, Salzburg*

74 The Serrarius' house, in which Mozart and his mother lived as guests during their visit to Mannheim from December 1777 to March 1778. Drawing of the house as it was before it was destroyed in 1943. *Reiss Museum, Mannheim*

75 Christoph Martin Wieland (1733–1813). Portrait by G. O. May, 1779. *Historisches Bildarchiv Handke*

77 Map of Paris (c. 1750). The detail shows the Rue du Gros Chenet where Mozart lived and where his mother died. *Institut Français, Munich*

78 Mozart's letter of 3rd July 1778 to Abbé Bullinger (1744 to c. 1788) who lived in Salzburg from 1775 to 1786 and was a good friend to him. *Mozarteum, Salzburg*

79 Medallion of Mozart's mother shown hanging on the wall in a family group painted by della Croce in 1780/1. *Mozarteum, Salzburg*

The Church of St Eustache. The façade was destroyed in 1688 and rebuilt in 1754/78. Picture of 1778. *Institut Français, Munich*

80 Final bars of the 'Turkish Rondo', the last movement of the piano sonata in A major (K. 331). This is the only remaining page of the original manuscript. *After a reproduction in the Mozarteum, Salzburg*

81 Louise d'Epinay (1725–1783) née Tardieu d'Eschavelles, mistress of Rousseau and Grimm. Painting by J. Etienne Liotard.

Page of an album in Mozart's hand (1778). *Sváz Ceskoslovenskych Skladatelu, Prague*

82 Aloysia Weber as Zémire in the opera *Azor et Zémire* by André Ernest Modeste Grétry (1742–1813), after an engraving by Johann Esaias Nilson. *Mozarteum, Salzburg*

Shrine of Maria Plain. *Museum Carolino-Augusteum, Salzburg*

83 Salzburg Cathedral, with its famous fountain, built by Santino Solari. *Photo: Frank*

84 Emanuel Schikaneder (1748–1812) in stage costume. After a silhouette by Ignaz Albrecht in his *Almanac for Theatre-Lovers*, 1791. *Austrian National Library, Vienna*

85 Mozart as an 'artist'. Ending of a letter of 10th May, 1779 to the 'little cousin'. *Mozarteum, Salzburg*

86 Burgstrasse, Munich, showing the Sonneck house (left of the gate) where Mozart stayed from November 1780 to March 1781 and finished *Idomeneo*. After a 19th-century water-colour by Otto Ruppert. *City Museum, Munich*

87 Dorothea Wendling (1737–1811), née Spurni, of French descent, married to the flautist Johann Baptist Wendling. She sang Elektra in *Idomeneo*. *Theatre Museum, Munich*

88 Title-page of an edition of *Idomeneo* of 1781. *Bavarian State Library, Munich*

89 Residenztheater, Munich. Longitudinal section by François Cuvilliés the Younger (1731–1777) of the auditorium in which the first performance of *Idomeneo* took place on 29th January 1781. Engraving by Valerian Funck after Cuvilliés' drawing in *Ecole de l'Architecture Bavaroise*, 1773. *Theatre Museum, Munich*

90 Emperor Josef II (1741–1790). *Austrian National Library, Vienna*

Josef and Aloysia Lange. After an engraving by Daniel Berger, 1786. *Mozarteum, Salzburg*

91 The house of the Teutonic Order in Vienna. *Austrian National Library, Vienna*

92 The Kärntnertor Theatre. After an engraving by J. E. Manfeld. *Austrian National Library, Vienna*

93 Katherine Cavalieri (1761–1801), born in Vienna, who created the rôle of Constanze in *Il Seraglio*. After a silhouette in Löschenkohl's *Austrian National Almanac*, 1786. *Austrian National Library, Vienna*

Valentin Adamberger (1743–1804) from Munich who came to Vienna via Venice. He created the role of Belmonte. After a silhouette by Löschenkohl, 1786. *Austrian National Library, Vienna*

Osmin's aria (last section) from *Il Seraglio*, in Mozart's writing. *Former Prussian State Library, Berlin*

94 Certificate of marriage, issued from St Stephen's, 4th August 1782. *Archives of St Stephen's, Vienna*

95 Ticket of admission to a 'dilettante concert' conducted by Mozart in the Augarten in 1782. *Mozarteum, Salzburg*

96 Franz Sales von Greiner (1732–1798) Mozart's friend. After an engraving by Mansfeld. *Austrian National Library, Vienna*

Nikolaus Joseph von Jacquin (1727–1798), a well-known botanist. Mozart was a close friend of all the Jacquin family, particularly the youngest son, Gottfried. Engraving by Jakob Adam, 1784, after the painting by Joseph Kreutzinger. *Austrian National Library, Vienna*

Gottfried van Swieten (1733-1803), patron of Haydn and Mozart. After an anonymous engraving. *Austrian National Library Vienna*

97 Johann Thomas von Trattnern (1717–1798). Engraving by Mansfeld (1781) after the painting by Joseph Hickel, 1770. *Austrian National Library, Vienna*

Johann Heinrich Müller (1738–1815), Court actor and dramatist, lived in Vienna from 1763. Engraving by Mansfeld after a painting by Weickhardt. *Austrian National Library, Vienna*

98 Kohlmarkt, Vienna. Engraving by C. Schütz, 1786. *Austrian National Library, Vienna*

99 Mozart by Josef Lange. Unfinished, oil on wood, 1782/3. *Mozarteum, Salzburg*

100 St Peter's, Salzburg. Roof and choir-loft with organ. *Photo: Frank*

101 Constanze Mozart (1762–1842), portrait by Josef Lange, 1782. *Mozarteum, Salzburg*

102 Mozart's sister, Nannerl, (1751–1829) in 1784. Anonymous painting, about 1785. *Mozarteum, Salzburg*

Nannerl's visiting card, written in her own hand, and one of her rings. *Mozarteum, Salzburg*

103 Mozart's list of his works, written in his own hand. The illustration shows the title-page. *Stefan Zweig estate*

No. 8 Schulergasse, Vienna, where Mozart composed *The Marriage of Figaro*. *Austrian National Library, Vienna*

104 Josef Haydn (1732–1809). Engraving based on a painting by John Hoppner, 1791. *Austrian National Library, Vienna*

105 Title-page of the first edition (1735) of the six string quartets (K. 387, 421, 428, 458, 464/5) of 1782/5 dedicated to Haydn. *Gesellschaft der Musikfreunde, Vienna*

106 Theatre in Schönbrunn Palace, after a watercolour by Rudolf von Alt, 1812–1905. *Austrian National Library, Vienna*

Mozart's list of his works: the items for 24th March and 29th April 1786. *Stefan Zweig estate*

107 Anna (Nancy) Selina Storace (1766–1817) who created the rôle of Susanna in *The Marriage of Figaro*. After a silhouette from Hieronymus Löschenkohl's *Austrian National Almanac*, 1786. *Mozarteum, Salzburg*

Lorenzo da Ponte (1748–1838), the librettist of *The Marriage of Figaro, Don Giovanni* and *Così fan Tutte*. From an engraving by M. Pettenino after a portrait by N. Rogers. *Mozarteum, Salzburg*

Michael Kelly (c. 1724–1826), the first Basilio in *Figaro*. After a silhouette by Löschenkohl, 1786. *Mozarteum, Salzburg*

108 Mozart. Relief in boxwood by Leonhard Posch, 1789. *Mozarteum, Salzburg*

109 Mozart's list of works; his entry for 10th August 1787, naming *Eine kleine Nachtmusik. Stefan Zweig estate*

Register of deaths of the church of St Andrea, Salzburg: the entry for Leopold Mozart's death on 28th May 1787. *Parish archives, St Andrea, Salzburg*

110 'Bertramka', the estate of the Duschek family, amongst the vineyards of Smichow near Prague, where Mozart wrote *Don Giovanni. Sváz Ceskoslovenskych Skladatelu, Prague*

111 Josepha Duschek, née Hambacher (1754–1824). Engraving by August Clar after a portrait by Haake, 1796. *Mozarteum, Salzburg*

112 Giacomo Casanova (1725–1788) after an engraving by J. Berka. Casanova was in Prague at the same time as Mozart. *Sváz Ceskoslovenskych Skladatelu, Prague*

Teresa Saporiti (1767–1869!), the first Donna Anna in *Don Giovanni*. After an engraving by Fambrini, 1791. *Mozarteum, Salzburg*

113 Playbill for the first performance of *Don Giovanni* in Prague. *Sváz Ceskoslovenskych Skladatelu, Prague*

Casanova's handwriting. Draft of the words of the sextet in Act 2 of *Don Giovanni*, written by him. *Sváz Ceskoslovenskych Skladatelu, Prague*

114 The 'Jupiter' Symphony in C Major (K. 551), 1788. Beginning of the first movement of Mozart's last symphony in his own writing. *Former Prussian State Library, Berlin*

Johanna Dorothea Stock (1760–1832), known as Doris Stock. Self-portrait in silverpoint, 1787. *Schillerhaus, Weimar*

115 Mozart (1789). His last portrait, a silverpoint drawing by Doris Stock. *Archives of the firm of Peters*

116 Leipzig. St. Thomas's Church seen from the town walls. Contemporary picture. *Municipal Museum, Leipzig*

18th-century picture of the Gewandhaus, Leipzig. *Municipal Museum, Leipzig*

Potsdam. The 'Bassin', where Mozart lived, after an 18th-century picture. *Historia Photo*

117 The old Burgtheater, Michaelerplatz, Vienna, where *Il Seraglio*, *Figaro* and *Così fan Tutte* received their first performances. After an engraving by Karl Postl. *Austrian National Library, Vienna*

118 *The Regensburg Diary or Weekly Announcements and News, 1790.* It announced Mozart's arrival in Regensburg. *Municipal Archives, Regensburg*

119 Programme of Mozart's concert in Frankfurt on 15th October 1790. *Historical Museum, Frankfurt*

120 Heinrich von Kleist (1777–1811) who saw *Don Giovanni* in Prague when he was fourteen. *Historia Photo*

121 Title-page of the libretto of *La Clemenza di Tito* (1791). *Sváz Ceskoslovenskych Skladatelu, Prague*

122 Josefa Hofer, née Weber (1758–1809), Mozart's sister-in-law, created the rôle of the Queen of the Night in *The Magic Flute*. After a silhouette. *Mozarteum, Salzburg*

123 Anna Gottlieb (1774–1856), Pamina in the first performance of *The Magic Flute*. After a silhouette. *Mozarteum, Salzburg*

125 Mozart's list of works: last page with the entry for 15th November 1791. *Stefan Zweig estate*

126 Entry in Haydn's diary recording Mozart's death. *Austrian National Library, Vienna*

127 The house where Mozart died in the Rauhensteingasse, Vienna (demolished in 1844 and replaced by the 'Mozarthof'). After a water-colour by E. Hutter. *Austrian National Library, Vienna*

128 The last notes Mozart wrote. The manuscript of the Requiem (K. 626) breaks off with the ninth bar of the Lacrymosa. The passage illustrated was followed by one bar of the soprano line alone. Only the first section was completed by Mozart, the rest being in skeleton score. The Sanctus, Benedictus and Agnus Dei are by Franz Xaver Süssmayr (1766–1803). *Austrian National Library, Vienna*

INDEX OF NAMES

Page numbers with an asterisk refer to illustrations